# SHOES

RIZZOLI
NEW YORK

# Colin McDowell

Preface by Manolo Blahnik

# SHOES

*Fashion and Fantasy*

*With 342 illustrations, 101 in colour*

*For Pilar Larrain del Solar*

First published in the United States of America in 1989 by
Rizzoli International Publications, Inc.
300 Park Avenue South, New York, NY 10010

Library of Congress Cataloging-in-Publication Data

McDowell, Colin.
Shoes: fashion and fantasy/Colin McDowell; with a preface by
Manolo Blahnik.
p. cm.
ISBN 0-8478-1112-3
1. Shoes. I. Title.
GT2130.M33 1989                    89-42808
391'.413–dc20                            CIP

Typeset in Linotype Fournier
Printed and bound in Italy by Amilcare Pizzi SpA, Milan

# CONTENTS

CHAPTER THREE

# FORM AND FUNCTION

97

Earliest footwear · Influence of the court on fashion · Impact of mass-production
Modern shoe types · Materials, fastenings and decorations
Recent influences on shoe fashions

CHAPTER FOUR

# SHOWBUSINESS AND RECREATIONAL FOOTWEAR

137

Shoes and the theatre · Dance shoes · Shoes in fancy dress, pantomime and the circus
The influence of Hollywood and popular music · Shoes and sport

CHAPTER FIVE

# THE DESIGNER AND THE DEVELOPMENT OF STYLE

177

The 20th century and the emergence of the great shoe designers · The influence of
mass-market manufacturers · The new designers · Fashionable developments
throughout the century

# SHOE DESIGN IS A

twentieth-century innovation. It was not until the early 1900s that the shoe designer as such came into being, and not until very recently indeed that young people studied shoemaking with the intention of entering the fashion world as shoe designers.

What has made this century the century of the shoe is, of course, as this book makes clear, the rise of couture and the birth of the shoe as fashion accessory. A fine shoe is now an essential part of fashionable dress. It can provide an accent to an outfit – whether witty, solemn, provocative or simply elegant. Dress designers know that the right shoes are a crucial ingredient to a successful look.

But the shoe designer did not always have the status in the fashion world that he has achieved today. The first shoemaker to achieve any fame at all was Yanturni, about whom nothing is known except that he was of Asian extraction and was the curator at the Cluny Museum in the early years of this century. I saw his work once, when I was very young, in an exhibition. I remember a Russian trunk full of shoes, brocaded, buckled, effortlessly elegant and light – everything seemed to be sustained by air. He was in love with rich materials (I share his fascination) and made shoes from all kinds of silks and antique laces.

Why or how Yanturni became a shoemaker, no one knows. André Perugia, the designer I admire most, was the son of a shoemaker – an accident of birth combined with extraordinary talent made him a great designer. Salvatore Ferragamo was apprenticed to a shoemaker at the age of eleven or thereabouts. Roger Vivier was at art school planning to be a sculptor when some friends invited him to design a collection of shoes.

I, too, became part of the world of shoes by complete chance. My mother had always designed her own shoes and used to have them made up by Don Cristino, the island shoemaker on Santa Cruz. I remember when I was a child, after the war, at a time when good leather and materials were very hard to get, my mother had wonderful ideas and used brocades and silks tied up in pieces of wood and leather. Naturally, I learnt from her. But I never thought that in the future I would be a designer.

I studied painting and literature and prepared a portfolio of fantastical drawings for theatre sets and costume designs. When I showed these to various people, to my great surprise everyone commented on the shoes.

Then began a complete visual education and an intense study of materials and leather. I visited factories, getting to know the machines and the people operating them and the way fashion works. I suppose I could have designed clothes or hats instead, but shoes somehow encapsulated most of what I have wanted to do as a designer. It is always a challenge to solve the problem that the foot presents: to achieve a proper balance between comfort, quality and design.

The inspiration for my own shoes has come from many sources: paintings, buildings and so on. From now on I shall also draw inspiration from this book, which has already afforded me hours of pleasure.

Yanturni made his shoes for very few hand-picked clients. It is not possible to do this today. Shoe designers have to produce for a market and to some extent the *craft* of shoemaking is dying. But interest in shoes is stronger than ever before and the 1980s has seen the birth of a new generation of shoemakers. Let us hope that some of these will develop into the Perugias and Viviers of the future.

# INTRODUCTION

*The view from the floor is of a pair of pointy black calf-height shoes, one of them twitching restlessly. . . . Then, later, a slightly more elevated view, from about two and a half feet above the floor . . . the gauzy cotton of her shirtwaist sleeves above a shorter skirt now and velvet pumps. . . . Still later, there is the view from about five feet above the floor: from here she is in high heels with rhinestone buckles. . . . A still later view: in the little Brooklyn house where she shuffles about in carpet slippers. . . .*

SO THE AMERICAN playwright, Arthur Miller, in his autobiography, *Timebends*, catalogues his relationship with his mother as he grows up and she grows old by describing her appearance, beginning always with her shoes.

Shoes are a very good starting point for several reasons. Not only do they reflect the personality of the wearer and, by the shapes they form through wear, tell how he or she walks and stands (in themselves quite strong indicators of personality), they also reveal the character by showing how the individual reacts to fashion. At the height of her powers, Miller's mother chooses power shoes, with high heels and shiny buckles, for visiting Broadway and taking in a show. When the Depression changes all that, and she has hit rock bottom, carpet slippers reflect her hopelessness. As he says, 'My mother moved with the times.'

For every Queen Mary, who wore the same shoe style throughout her entire reign, or Max Beerbohm, who, even when lying gravely ill, was still enough the dandy to greet a visitor with, 'Tell me, is Lobb still the best bootmaker in London?', there are millions who see shoes as nothing more permanent or important than an item of clothing destined to last for two or three years at the most and then to be forgotten like any other fashion. Of course, fashion is fugitive: at the very moment that a style becomes fashionable it begins to die. And yet, how many of us keep shoes that we know will almost certainly never be worn again but which we cannot bear to part with? What is it that makes shoes often seem so much more personal than other articles of clothing?

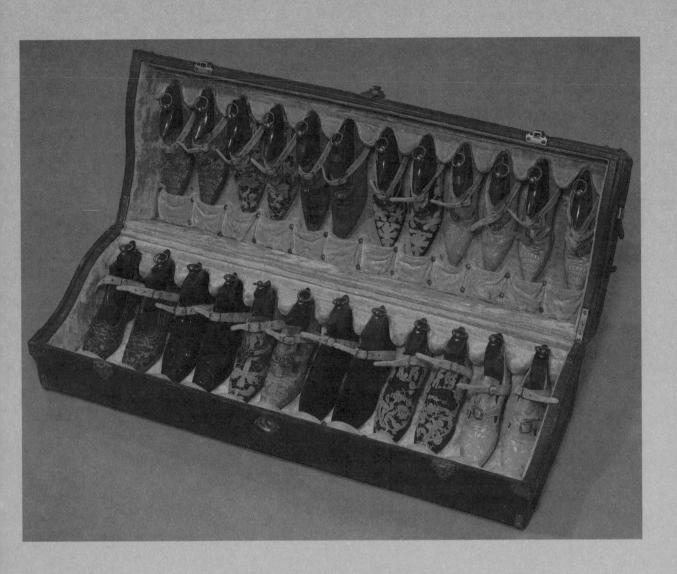

Trunk containing shoes made
by Yanturni for Rita de Acosta
Lydig, c.1914-19

Obviously, for many people it has to do with comfort, which brings with it a sense of well-being. The joy of wearing light-as-a-breeze shoes was captured by Ira Gershwin in his song in *The Berkeleys of Broadway*: 'When I've got shoes with wings on, the town is full of rhythm and the world's in rhyme, and living has no strings on.' It was sung, appropriately enough, by wing-footed Fred Astaire.

These days we take comfort for granted but for the majority of people well-fitting footwear became possible only with the advent of mass-production, which evolved in its modern sense in the United States at the end of the nineteenth century. Life is not only a matter of comfort, however, and it is not the fit of shoes but their style that can give us the feeling that we have wings on even if, in reality, we are being crippled. Like all clothes, shoes affect our self-esteem. If they are stylish, we feel stylish, and to hell with comfort. In the eighteenth-century poem, 'Monsieur à la Mode', the gallant wore a smart pair of pumps 'made up of grained leather, so thin he can't venture to tread on a feather'. One can guarantee that as each stone cut through his wafer-thin sole, the gentleman felt no pain, buoyed up as he was by the euphoria of knowing that he was cutting a fashionable figure.

Today the search for style has taken over from the desire to be fashionable. The ultimate effect of fashion is to make everyone look alike; having style means accepting the broad flow of fashion but making it individual to oneself. One way in which people have tried to 'personalize' their appearance is by having their shoes made uniquely to their specification – a luxury reserved only for the very rich. But for those who could afford it, exotic footwear was a marvellously self-indulgent way of looking distinguished. On New Year's Day 1584, Sir Philip Sidney gave to Queen Elizabeth I 'A paire of slippers of black vellat all over embrodered with venys gold, perle and smale garnets.' They sound so delicate and exquisite, how could the queen fail to feel pampered and privileged when she slipped them on?

The joys of magnificence are still with us in this century. It is not hard to imagine the feelings of luxury with which the socialite Nancy Lancaster removed the cherry shoe-trees from her Yanturni pumps of deep crimson Genoese velvet, embroidered all over with gold leaf and sporting a huge diamond buckle. The shoes probably fitted perfectly but, if they didn't, would she care? The singer Lily Pons so loved her shoes that she had Louis Vuitton make her a secretaire with individual drawers for each pair in order to protect them during travel.

Both sexes require comfort in their shoes but they do not wish to sacrifice too much style and fashion awareness to it. They feel that it should be possible to have smart footwear and still be able to walk with ease. Apart from shoes that are badly made or which do not fit, the greatest cause of discomfort is the high heel, which forces the foot forward in the shoe. This discomfort has been happily ignored by men as well as women in the past. The high heel is a fashion that has hovered between the sexes over the centuries.

At this point in our fashion evolution the high heel is seen as an almost exclusively feminine shoe type, but this was not the case in the 1970s and surely will not permanently be the situation in the future. The briefest glance over the history of shoes will reveal that high heels have had a potent appeal for men in terms of both fashion and practicality.

The history of footwear is inextricably linked to the history of transport. For every century but our own, the commonest means of getting from one place to another have been walking or riding. Horse-riding, for pleasure or transport, has been an overwhelmingly masculine prerogative and this fact has had a considerable effect on the design of heels for men's shoes. High heels for men helped keep the foot in the stirrup and aided control of the horse during hard riding. They could not be functional if the heel was too narrow and tapering, as it would be liable to snap; and if it were too high, walking was difficult. So male high heels were a response to a practical need; they had to be dual-purpose, suitable for riding and convenient for walking.

The lessons of putting fashion before practicality had been learned early on: at the battle of Sempach in 1386, Austrian knights who wished to dismount and continue the skirmish on foot could not walk in their excessively long, pointed iron shoes until the armourers had snapped off the tips. Fashion quickly gives way to the urge for self-preservation.

Men's boots had high heels until the middle of the nineteenth century when, with improved coach design and the development of the railways, there was less demand for a boot designed to be pre-eminently suitable for riding. Women's high heels were equally a reflection of their mode of transport. The vast majority of women's shoes that have survived from past centuries are of a delicacy and magnificence that make it clear that they were not made to be worn out of doors. A remarkably high proportion of them are in satin and brocade, often elaborately embroidered; very few are of leather or any material sturdy enough to withstand the filth of the streets. When women travelled they went by coach or, during the

High-heeled lady's shoe from the reign of Louis XIV

seventeenth century, by sedan chair – an invention that revolutionized town transport. A woman could arrive at her destination comparatively safely and certainly clean shod in her sedan – at Versailles sedans were carried directly into the public rooms so that ladies might alight onto dry, clean floors.

Obviously, practicality has little to do with female high heels. They have always been essentially about allure – as they are today. In the eighteenth century a wag made fun of the tyranny of high heels with his couplet addressed to fashion victims: 'Mount on French heels when you go to a ball, it now is the fashion to totter and fall'. And indeed, at the court of Louis XVI, women wore such extreme high heels that they could walk only with the aid of a stick and could not tackle stairs without the help of an admirer, servant or, if all else failed, a husband. The female high heel was curved and tilted to make women look precious and provocative – in much the same way as high heels do today.

Of course, we are talking about a tiny proportion of any country's population when we discuss the expensive clothing of the ultra-fashionable. For the majority of people footwear was chosen (if indeed there was any choice) for practicality. Working men and women wanted boots that kept the wet out and the warmth in; they could not wear anything that did not answer to their practical needs and certainly would not modify those needs in the interests of sex appeal. By the very nature of their different lives, it is always easier to chart sartorial change in the upper classes than in the workers, whose shoes are normally worn to the death, but this does not mean that the working classes were unaware of fashionable developments. Ladies' maids frequently received their mistresses' cast-offs (provided they were not too decorative) and, in common with the footman, were given shoes as part of their wages. Even though working-class shoes were simple and decent rather than costly and exquisitely made, they usually shared the fashion features of the shoes of the better-off.

The differences between the rich and privileged on one hand and the poor and deprived on the other were to be entirely swept away by the French Revolution – or so it was hoped. To a certain degree, they were. After the revolutionary fanaticism of the Terror, a period of republican dignity was introduced during the Directoire, from 1795 to 1799. Republican ideals were based on simplicity and in fashion the role model was Greece. Pseudo-Grecian dress was in dramatic contrast to the clothes worn in pre-revolutionary France. No more were rich brocades and sumptuous satins required; the plain high-waisted dresses that took their place were softly diaphanous. The new shoes were as plain: flat, without heels, and tied with criss-cross ribbons. Men's shoes were also flat, with smaller heels. The fashion spread to other parts of Europe and Pückler Muskau noticed when he visited London that men and women were wearing 'shoes as light as paper, which are freshly varnished every day'.

Changes in fashion do not simply affect modes; they also have a profound influence on manners. One of the most interesting and lasting effects of fashion shoes of the Directoire period was on the way in which people walked. The characteristic courtier's walk of the Rococo age was puppet-like and stilted. High heels gave even the most masculine of men a slightly mincing gait and women looked as though they were gliding on wheels. With the low-heeled shoes of the Directoire, the modern walk was born. Aristocrats (there were still quite a few left, despite the Terror) and upper gentry for the first time in generations walked naturally and easily, as peasants and children had always done.

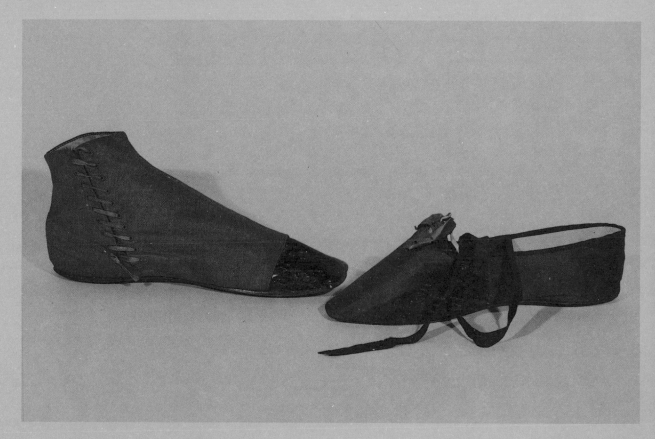

When they were not walking, they were dancing – a mania for public balls swept Paris and fanned out to take in the rest of Europe at the same time as militarism was also engulfing the continent. War has always been glamorous; Napoleon made it chic. With him began the movement to have soldiers bedecked in magnificent uniforms and equipage, a movement which continued up to the Boer War. He even allowed his marshals to design their own uniforms. An officer's boots had to be the very perfection of his authority – immaculately made and beautifully kept. His men were scarcely less superbly shod. Bagehot, in his *English Constitution*, sets out the equation. 'The soldier – that is, the great soldier – of today is not a romantic animal', he wrote, 'but a quiet, grave man . . . thinking, as the Duke of Wellington was said to do, *most* of the shoes of his soldiers.'

Wars have never stopped balls and they did not do so in the nineteenth century. They were taken very seriously. Since women's dance shoes were as delicate as modern ballet slippers and the new dancing was much more vigorous than the old minuets, it was common enough for popular girls to wear out a pair of shoes before the evening was over. Many carried an extra pair in case they danced through the soles.

Women's dance slippers have continued to take a lot of punishment. Lady Diana Cooper remembered that when she was a girl her pale satin shoes were smudged by clumsy male feet before the first dance was over but, as a nineteenth-century manual of etiquette put it, 'a ball is too formal a place for anyone to indulge in personal preference', and the massacre of one's shoes had to be borne with stoicism.

The deadening hand of gentility and respectability was laid on all aspects of life as the Victorian age developed. Middle-class morality swept away the sultry and voluptuous Byronic romanticism which had begun the century. Smouldering passions and exquisite melancholy were blown away like so much mist by the tradesman attitudes that dominated Victorian England. Overriding all other

Woman's pump in brown silk with bow and crossed ribbons, Stockholm, 1830. *Left:* Woman's flat ankle boot in beige cotton, Germany, *c.*1830

*Une Tournure à faire tourner toutes les têtes!,* lithograph by Charles Vernier, 1858

considerations was the desire to protect women from passion – their own as well as men's. As the century moved on, it became manifest that the well-bred woman could not be acknowledged to possess anything as base and potentially carnal as legs. At the most, all that could be seen was a demurely clothed toe occasionally peeping out from beneath heavy skirts.

This was a highly unsatisfactory state of affairs for both men and women but hope was aroused with the invention of what surely must be one of the most impractical fashions ever to gain wide currency. The crinoline was, by any standards, ridiculous – but it was also seductive. The steel hoops that buoyed out the skirt kept it in a state of endless movement. The slightest pressure at one point raised it correspondingly at the opposite point, often revealing a titillating and tantalizing glimpse of the forbidden flesh – the female ankle.

In an era when womanhood was put on a pedestal and yet endlessly hunted after, the crinoline was the ideal garment. Its 'do not touch' exterior was so constantly being pushed up to expose the woman below that a new fashion in footwear soon evolved. The simple pump disappeared and the ankle boot took its place. It can be argued that the boot was meant to calm men's fevered thoughts by encasing the female flesh. What in fact happened was that the boots, with their high heels and tight lacing, were so erotically charged that they made the crinoline an extremely provocative garment, enjoyed by men and understood by women.

The beginning of the twentieth century saw an enormous increase in styles and colours in women's shoes. It was at this time that the United States started to pull ahead in producing fashionable shoes to a level of style not found in British or European mass-produced footwear. By the twenties America had established a comfortable lead and it kept it throughout the thirties and forties. The American author Margaret Halsey pinpointed the difference when she wrote, 'Englishwomen's shoes look as if they had been made by someone who had often heard shoes described but had never seen any.' It was a judgment hard to refute until well after World War II.

Modern fashion has been predominantly a female affair. Men's appearance became increasingly standardized as the nineteenth century developed and, by the beginning of the twentieth, had virtually become a uniform. This is especially true of men's shoes. In all, there were only three or four styles, which looked identical from a distance.

Since the 1960s men have become a lot more adventurous as social and sexual stereotypes have become looser but they still lack the originality shown by twentieth-century women. Since 1900 women's shoes have embraced more variations than in the whole previous history of dress. Shoe designers have taken styles from every period of history, including those worn by men, and developed them to coincide with contemporary fashion moods. They have played games with scale, proportion, colour and texture. It is not an exaggeration to say that some of the most perfect shoes ever produced have been created in this century by great designers who have no equals from the past.

Even more important is the general level of shoe design for the masses. Never before have people been shod in such well-designed shoes that give comfort as well as style at prices affordable to all. There is, however, a potential danger for the twenty-first century. When Joseph William Foster founded the first sports shoe company in the early 1890s, which became Reebok in 1958 when his grandson took over the firm, could he have imagined how important athletic footwear would become to non-athletic life? It would be a sad thing if shoe design were diminished to variations on the trim of sneakers. Shoes can lift the spirits, delight the soul and give confidence to the insecure. And though no one can doubt that increased informality is beneficial in every area of life, the dangers of universal casualness must be acknowledged. Well-designed shoes which are witty and original can, like all good design, enhance the quality of life. Perhaps we should heed the warning implied in Lord Palmerston's letter to Littleton in 1829: ' . . . your Mustaphas have no idea of any traffic beyond rhubarb, figs and red slippers; but what energy can be expected from a nation who have no heels to their shoes and pass their whole life slipshod?'

*Overleaf*
*Left:* Classical statue of Mercury in Repose, from Herculaneum
*Right:* Stephen Linard, Winged Shoes, 1988

Women's travelling and walking shoes, 1892

# VIRTUOSO VIVIER

*Roger Vivier is the king of the decorative shoe. Although his creations catch the spirit of previous eras, they are completely contemporary: always fashion and never costume.*

*Vivier has been designing shoes for more than fifty years and his influence on younger shoemakers is unmatched.*

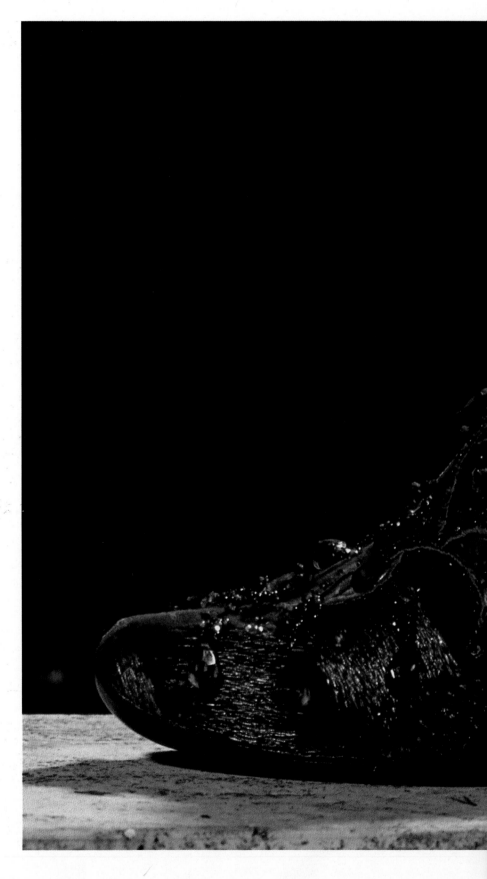

Shoe by Roger Vivier, 1987

# U.S. STYLE

*David Evins has designed shoes for almost every woman in American public life over the past forty years. He has lasts of the feet of all of the great and the good, including the politicians' wives and the famous film stars, and for years he was a favourite of that most demanding of fancy dressers, the Duchess of Windsor.*

*He had the honour of designing the Inaugural shoes for Mrs Ronald Reagan in 1980 and 1984 and has worked on collections of shoes to accompany the designs of many of America's top designers. Many of his clients admit that what appeals to them about Evins shoes is the fact that they are classic designs, well-made and comfortable.*

*Precisely the same claim would be made by the owners of the exclusive handcrafted shoes designed for the past twenty years by Susan Bennis and Warren Edwards. The ranks of their discerning customers have been described as reading like an amalgam of Oscar nominees, Billboard's Top Ten and the Social Register. Whether they are designed for men or for women, Bennis-Edwards shoes have an originality that sets them apart.*

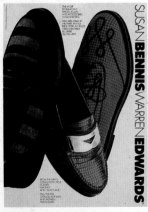

*Left:* Shoes by Susan Bennis and Warren Edwards, 1988

*Top right:* David Evins shoe for the Duchess of Windsor, 1950s

*Centre right:* David Evins shoe for the Duchess of Windsor, 1950s

*Lower right:* David Evins shoes for Mrs Ronald Reagan: 1st Inaugural shoe, 1980; 2nd Inaugural shoe, 1984

*Main picture:* David Evins boot for Marlene Dietrich, Galanos Collection, 1953

# BUCKLED BLAHNIK

*Manolo Blahnik's buckled evening extravaganza is extrovert enough to excite Alexander the Great and its lucky wearer will be making a statement that has nothing whatever to do with the timorous and self-effacing picture so often conjured up by the word sandal. These are in satin with pearl and diamond buckles and their natural surroundings are the ballroom on a private yacht or a boudoir for an intimate supper* à deux.

*The buckles from the Lady Maufe Collection must surely have lifted the spirits of their privileged wearers in the eighteenth century in much the same way as Blahnik's do today.*

*Above:* Georgian shoe buckles from the Lady Maufe Collection

*Right:* Manolo Blahnik sandal, 1989

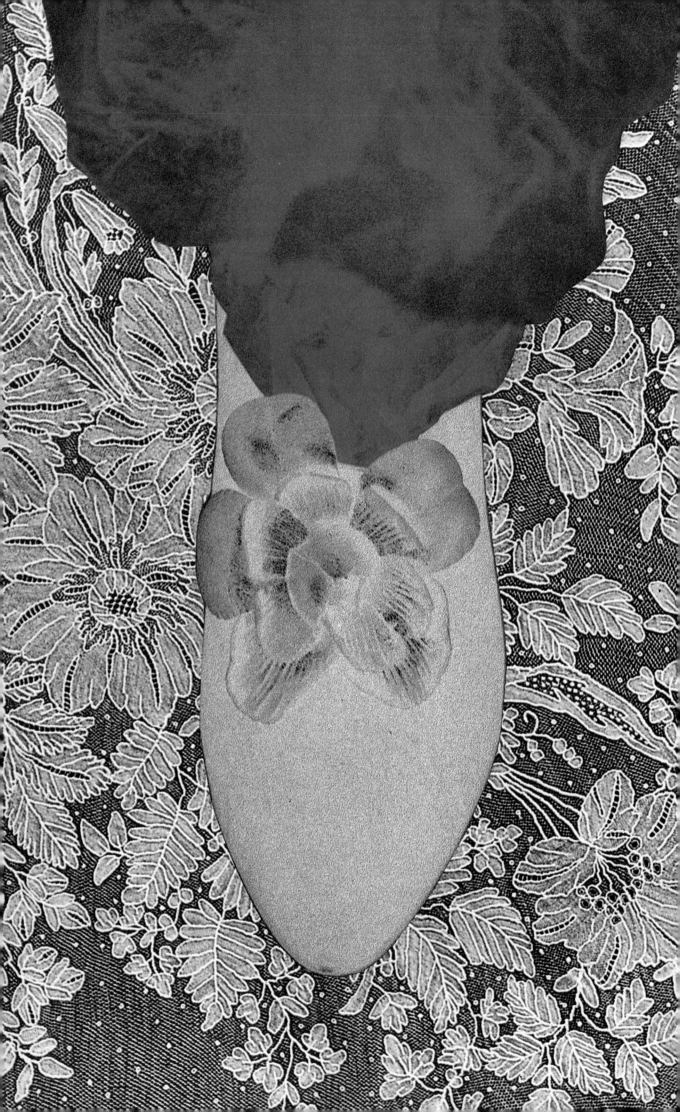

# THE SHOE AND THE SHOEMAKER

SHOES WHICH FIT well are a modern luxury. According to one of London's most famous bootmakers, even in the first few decades of the twentieth century a grand customer insisted on his valet wearing his new bespoke shoes for six months to 'break them in' and make them comfortable. If hand-made shoes required this sort of treatment, it is not hard to imagine the skinned heels, chafed toes and bunions that resulted from the new, unseasoned and coarse leather that was used for cheaper boots and shoes.

Late-nineteenth-century periodicals and newspapers were full of advertisements for preparations to undo the damage caused by ill-fitting footwear. The magnitude of the problem can be gauged from the masses of cures for corns which promised 'to obviate the necessity for the knife'. Some of these seem unconvincing to modern eyes. Highly recommended were a paste made from the 'common house leek' and one using 'common soda of the oil-shops' placed on buff leather sticking plaster.

C & J Clark, the Somerset shoemakers, tried to solve the problem at source. In 1833 they advertised boots and shoes manufactured on anatomical principles

Shoe by Martine Sitbon, 1988

and promised that 'these boots do not deform the feet or cause corns and bunions, but are comfortable to wear and make walking a pleasure'.

However, it was not badly made shoes alone that caused problems. Many of the difficulties arose as a result of the widespread cult of the tiny foot, seen at its most extreme in China, where footbinding was common until well into this century. The Western correlation of small feet with high birth and sexual desirability is precisely the same as that of the Chinese; only the degree of cultural emphasis is different.

The roistering California gold rush song about Darlin' Clementine makes it clear that the assumption that small feet were a mark of superior breeding was a common one, and was not confined to the middle and upper classes. The rough and ready prospectors who roared out the chorus, 'Herring boxes without topses, sandals were for Clementine', were poking fun at a girl with such enormous feet ('number nine') that she was ungainly and devoid of feminine charm. Even in the world of the 'forty niners', where women were scarce, the ideal of the petite foot was kept alive. It is still current in this century, which is why 'Fats' Waller had a great success with his song, 'Your Feet's Too Big.'

The Western anatomy is not the same as that of the East. Big-boned, large feet are common in both sexes. It is not surprising, therefore, that the opposite, the small and narrow foot, has been the ideal for a long time. In all periods some fashionable women have been ready to bind their feet in ribbons or gauze bandages in order to make them appear smaller. Even today, many women attempt a *trompe l'oeil* trick by wearing shoes that are a size too small.

It is not only women who prize a small foot. Petrarch is reputed to have almost lamed himself in shoes that were too small in order to 'display to his Laura a neat foot'. Dandies, described by Carlyle as men 'whose trade, office and existence consists in the wearing of clothes', have frequently bound their feet and fashionable men have regularly bought shoes that were too small for them. The elegant and sophisticated Fred Astaire, who could surely be considered a modern dandy, is reputed to have worn his dancing shoes half a size too small.

Chinese woman's shoe, *c*.1900, approximately lifesize

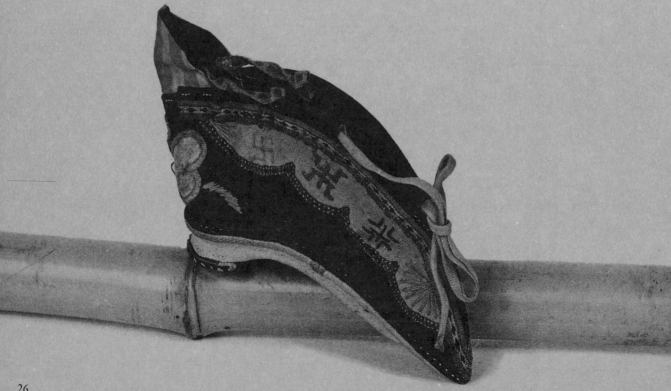

Practicality in footwear, which has always been important for workers, has rarely been the major consideration with the more favoured classes, for whom appearance has been paramount. Many extreme shoe styles from the past show that comfort has been given barely a thought by keen followers of fashion. One of the most disagreeable shoes to wear must have been the peaked shoe, known as the poulaine or crackowe, because of its Polish origin. Long and tapering, it could be worn with ease only by someone with an exceedingly narrow foot. A normal set of toes would literally have needed to be crunched one on top of the other. And yet this bizarre style was popular throughout Europe with men of all but the lowest labouring classes for several decades in the twelfth and fifteenth centuries.

Churchmen condemned it as lewd and provocative, and indeed it was. The long toe was clearly phallic, even more so when padded with horse hair and curled up at the tip. A young blood enjoyed sliding a foot under a woman's skirts as he sat opposite her at table or, with his friends on the street corners, waggling his toes suggestively as the girls walked by. It is not surprising that a Papal bull of 1468, condemning the poulaine as 'a scoffing against God and the church, a worldyly vanity and a mad presumption', had little effect. The bull attempted to limit the length of the toe but, as a contemporary chronicler records, 'sum men sayd that they wold were long pykys whethyr Pope wylle or nylle, for they sayde the Popys curse wolde not kylle a fly'.

In the end, like all fashions, the poulaine became the victim of its own popularity. Once it was so universal that, as Monstrelet wrote, 'even boys, especially in the courts of princes, had points at the toes of their shoes a quarter of an ell long', the fashionable had to move on. The swing away from the narrow style could hardly have been more complete. Its place was taken by the broad-toed shoe so familiar from Holbein's paintings.

Although comfortable and accommodating, the broad shoe was not glamorous. Even when slashed across the vamp to reveal lining of silk and satin, it had no chic, as the common names for it – cow's mouth and duck's bill – make clear. But, as is the way with fashion, the new shoe, being so different from what had gone before, found favour. This rejection and acceptance is the rhythm of fashion. In this century, the swing from thin delicate silhouettes to thick strong shapes – one of the basic movements responsible for developments in fashion – was repeated almost identically when the stiletto heel and pointed toe were replaced by the platform sole and thick heel.

*Left:* The pointed shoe, *c.*1470.
*Right:* The broad shoe, *c.*1485.
Engravings by Israel Van Meckenem

Venetian courtesan wearing
chopines, 1592

The poulaine in its most extreme form had been predominantly a male mode, but men were not alone in ignoring comfort and practicality and slavishly following fashion. Early sixteenth-century Venice produced the most extreme shoe style ever seen, a style that was eagerly taken up by the more adventurous of the city's women. The chopine, a shoe on an inordinately high platform sole, was as ungainly as it was uncomfortable. Travellers marvelled. Thomas Coryat wrote in his *Crudities* (1611) that the fashion was

> so common in Venice that no woman whatever goeth without it, either in her house or abroad . . . so uncomely a thing, in my opinion, that it is a pity this foolish custom is not clean banished . . . there are many of these chapineys of a great height even half a yard high . . . by how much the nobler a woman is, by so much the higher are her chapineys. All their gentlewomen . . . are assisted and supported either by men or women, when they walk abroad, to the end they might not fall.

For once the Church did not rush to condemn. A contemporary commentator suggested that the chopine had been invented by jealous Italian husbands who hoped that the cumbersome movement it entailed would make illicit liaisons difficult. The fashion was a gift to writers: Raymond's *Voyage Through Italy* (1648) referred to 'walking maypoles'; the traveller Douce decided that 'Venetian ladies are made of three things, one part wood, meaning the chapins, another part was their apparel and the third part was a woman.' It is not easy to say for certain how far the fashion spread beyond Venice but, like most extreme styles, it was probably more talked about than worn.

The chopine did have a more practical counterpart – the patten – widely used well into the middle of the nineteenth century and, in some rural districts, as late as the 1920s. Early pattens were made of a shaped wooden block of perhaps two inches in height into which the foot, wearing a shoe, could be placed. This construction enabled people to walk without sinking into the mud. In their commonest form, pattens had an iron ring fixed to the sole to give height with lightness. The word patten, the universality of which is shown by the fact that it has more than twenty-five different spellings, was largely interchangeable with the word galoshe, which has at least thirteen spellings ranging from galoche to gallegege.

Despite its universality, the origin of the word patten is obscure. It is possibly linked to the old French word, *patte*, meaning a paw, but the most attractive view of how the word came into being was suggested by John Gay. In his poem 'The Implements for Walking the Streets, and Signs of the Weather', Gay tells the tale of Patty, the only daughter of a Lincolnshire yeoman, who was so loved by the god Vulcan that he, having seen how 'Deep through the miry lane she pick'd her way, Above her ankle rose the chalky clay', invented the patten – 'which from the blue-ey'd Patty takes the name' – in order to keep his 'pale virgin' out of the mud.

It is not difficult to see why virtually every countrywoman and her children used pattens. Until country roads were metalled, in the nineteenth century, they were virtually impassable in the winter. An entry in Pepys's diary for November 1665 describes the hazard: 'It was horrible foule weather; and my lady Batten walking through the dirty lane with new spicke and span white shoes, she dropped one of her galoshes in the dirt, where it stuck, and so forced to go home with one, at which she was horribly vexed . . . '

Pattens were also necessary in town, where the noise from their metal rings caused some irritation. In *Northanger Abbey*, Jane Austen describes Lady Russell 'entering Bath on a wet afternoon amidst the dash of other carriages . . . and the ceaseless clink of pattens . . . ' Within living memory, a notice outside Hawkesbury Church in Gloucestershire, England, requested that 'persons that do come to this church would be careful to leave their dogs at home and that women would not walk in with their pattens'.

Equally practical, and universal with workers in town or country, were clogs. Like pattens, they survived well into the twentieth century as everyday footwear and are still worn in certain trades.

Although clogs and wooden-soled shoes have had their brief moments in fashion, their wear has been traditionally confined to the poor and those whose jobs demand extra-tough or protective footwear. The mill workers of the northwest of England, for example, wore them for safety on factory floors which were frequently wet and greasy. The clog that evolved in the United States and Great Britain differed from the Continental version. In the main, the French sabot, Dutch clog and German *Klomp* were all made from a single block of wood, whereas American and British clogs were constructed like a shoe – that is, with a separate wooden sole and leather upper.

Pair of women's pattens with raised arch and iron ring, c.1760s

The wood traditionally chosen for handcarved clogs was alder, though birch, sycamore and willow were also used. Machine-made clogs are mostly made of birch because alder splits when the machine cuts against the grain. In the past, itinerant craftsmen known as bodgers prepared wood for clogs, from the cutting to the rough shaping of the wood into soles. The soles were stacked in pyramids so that the air could circulate around them to ensure natural and even drying. Modern factory methods have hardly changed the making of clogs except that the shaping and drying of the wood are no longer done outdoors. One of the essentials of a good pair of clogs is that they are paired at birth so that they shrink in the drying process to the same extent.

The fight against dirt and the need for protection was not confined to the working classes. It was a problem for everybody until metalled roads were developed. Bad weather turned country roads into quagmires and even city streets were filthy with the litter and waste of a growing population which had no sanitary methods of disposal. The search for suitably elegant protection for the fashionable against the filth underfoot produced a shoe known as the 'slap sole' in the seventeenth century. This was a flat extension of the sole, on which the high heel of a shoe rested. The principle was the same as the eskimo's snow shoe, in that the sole forced the mud aside and prevented the heel from sinking into the dirt. The slap sole was an expensive addition. It is seen at its most magnificent on the boots of Henry Rich and the First Duke of Hamilton in their portraits by Mytens, but it was also frequently worn by women.

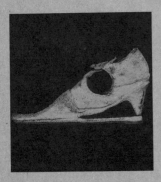

Woman's shoe with slap sole, 1660-80

All design development comes from one of two sources. It is normally the result of changes in practical needs but it is also often stimulated by the fashionable desire to have something different. The most momentous and far-reaching change in shoes must surely be the development of the raised heel. Although created for protection against dirty streets, it was also very definitely a response to a change in fashion mood. The theory that the heel evolved for men because they needed it to keep their foot in the stirrup is hotly debated by scholars, many of whom maintain that horse-riding peoples in the Middle East did not require heels any more than warlike races such as the Tartars.

The origins of the female heel are as contentious. The chopine brought to the notice of Europe the advantages of raising the foot from the ground. However, chopines were heavy and cumbersome. Even in the East, from which the style had come, this problem had been recognized and many chopines were made with the sole hollowed out in the middle, to create a shoe on stilts. When the chopine spread from Venice across Europe as a *succès fou*, its advantages in practical and fashion terms were obvious – but so were its disadvantages.

The chopine severely limited mobility and forced the wearer to adopt a somewhat comical way of walking. However, it soon became apparent that by lowering the sole at the front both problems could be solved. So the heel was created. It was an immediate success and, with only the briefest of eclipses, has remained in fashion ever since. The heel spelled the demise of the concept of shaping each shoe to the foot: in other words, of having a right and a left shoe. Shoemakers at this time found it uneconomic to make the enormous quantity of lasts required to produce shoes which would have a heel and also be shaped for each foot. They and the fashionable opted for the heels. Shaped shoes disappeared until the nineteenth century, when the development of the pantograph made it possible to make mirror-image lasts in quantity.

Although the thinking that produced the sixteenth-century high heel was similar to that behind the chopine, the similarity ended there. Because the new style was meant to confer dignity, there was never any question of making it so high that walking might prove hazardous, but the opportunity to add 2 inches to one's height was eagerly taken by those whose position in society required them to look imposing. Louis XIV was a mere 5 foot 5½ inches tall and must have felt a completely different man when he put on his high-heeled shoes as part of the panoply of his power as Sun King. He is known frequently to have worn heels as high as 4½ or 5 inches which were often decorated with miniature paintings of battles or classical idylls.

Like most of the royal heads of Europe, Louis XIV adopted red as the colour of kingship: his wooden heels were covered in red leather and this distinctive fashion quickly spread to his courtiers. Red heels were one of the few seventeenth-century fashions to appear in England before being seen in France: James I had favoured them since the beginning of the century and they became firmly established for court dress.

It was at this time that the fantastic form of decoration known as the shoe rose became a craze in aristocratic circles. Louis XIII of France is reputed to be the first monarch to wear shoe roses, but it was in later reigns that they became breathtakingly ostentatious. As early as 1588 Philip Stubbes, in *The Anatomy of Abuses*, had commented on the shoes of fashionable folk, 'stitched with silk and embroidered with gold and silver all over the foot with gew-gaws innumerable'. The extravagance was continued in the roses worn throughout the next century, of which Roger Bacon wrote, 'Now ribbon-roses take such place that garden-roses want their grace.'

The desire for luxury and the determination to cut a fine figure caused courtiers to spend very considerable amounts of money on their shoe roses, as they did on all other aspects of their dress for important occasions. John Taylor put it into perspective when he wrote that men were now willing to 'wear a farm in shoe strings edged with gold, and spangled garteres worth a copy-hold'.

Up to the seventeenth century, footwear had been virtually identical for both sexes although because women wore long skirts, which hid their feet, their shoes were less extravagantly decorated than men's. Except for riding, women only rarely wore boots. Indeed, it seems that even as riding equipment they were relatively uncommon. In June 1666 Pepys notes his surprise at meeting in Whitehall ladies 'dressed in their riding garb with boots and doublets, just for all the world like mine'.

For seventeenth-century men, however, boots were *the* glamour footwear and they remained so for more than two hundred years. Although they changed shape, were sometimes higher and sometimes wider, their message did not alter. It

Louis XIV as the Sun King

Early 20th-century advertisement for Barthman Schuhe

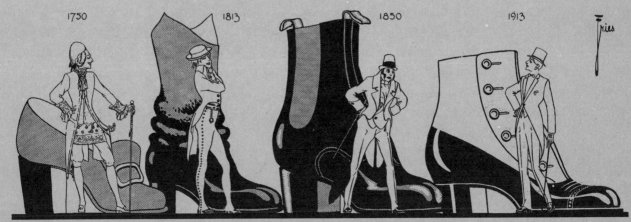

1750    1813    1850    1913

*Shoeing Asses.* Caricature by I. Cruikshank, 1807

was, as it is today, a simple, even crude, one. Boots were macho. They made men want to swagger; they brought into the domestic scene overtones of hard riding, mighty battles and close male companionship. They were as chauvinist as the codpiece. The occasional tough woman might wear masculine-style boots for riding, but she was an exception.

The difference between men's and women's footwear – and the attitudes it provoked – was seen most clearly from this time on by the way men increasingly wore boots and women were left with decorative shoes which limited their mobility. For women, a brief trip out of doors became an event. Pattens had to be fixed if the weather was bad or conditions underfoot were poor. This meant that walking any great distance was difficult and doing so quickly was impossible. Pepys describes an outing with his wife when she was 'exceedingly troubled with a new pair of pattens', and pronounces himself 'vexed to go so slow'.

As the seventeenth century progressed, men's shoes became increasingly suitable for both indoor and outdoor wear and women's shoes remained appropriate only for indoors. By mid-century, the slippers, pantoufles and mules worn by women had grown increasingly decorative. Made of fine silks and satins, richly embroidered and using the latest colours, they were indisputably gorgeous. One of their distinctive design features, which carried on into the eighteenth century, was a white kid rand running between the sole and the shoe. It was a demarcation line in more senses than one. Shoes like these could never have been subjected to the rough and tumble of foul streets and this again raises the question of just how housebound women were.

Certainly, from this period until late Victorian times, women's shoes became less and less able to cope with conditions out of doors. Brocade, velvet and tapestry shoes, frequently embroidered to match a dress, have survived in so much greater numbers than leather shoes that it must be assumed that the latter were exceptional for women. A comment by Daniel Defoe in 1725 gives a further clue. He remarks of a country girl brought up to London to be a servant in a fashionable house that 'her neat leathern shoes are now transformed into laced ones'. Perhaps workmanlike leather shoes were considered *déclassé* by the woman of fashion, who saw them as an item essentially for the wives of the yeoman and tradesman classes.

During the eighteenth century, men's boots became refined and slimmed down; they had turned-down tops, lined in brown, contrasting with the black leather of the rest of the boot, and were based on the boots worn by jockeys for the newly fashionable sport of horse racing. In fact, the *Universal Spectator* in 1739 refers to 'sparks who choose to appear as jockeys, seldom to be seen without boots'.

Although men wore boots and shoes that were becoming increasingly practical tools for living the active life, they did not entirely turn their backs on pattern and colour. Black and brown were the favourite colours but tan and pale shades were by no means uncommon among the gentry. At home they wore slippers and mules of embroidered silk and brocade. The man of fashion, a recognized historical type, took infinite care over his appearance, and boots and shoes were high on the list of things which had to be absolutely correct. Not only must they conform to the latest fashionable developments, they must also be immaculately kept. In some cases, idleness and self-involvement transformed a sensible interest in appearance into foppish over-concern.

Restoration comedies are full of fops whose obsessions are gossip, sex and their appearance, and their type continues throughout the Georgian period. The Grand Tour had its effect. Dandified young men returned to England so suffused with their superiority as travelled persons that they determined to be as different as possible from the bumpkins who had stayed at home. Affecting foreign mannerisms, speech and habits, they were a gift to the satirists who christened them Macaronis and mercilessly parodied them. So determined were Macaronis to draw attention to themselves in London streets that they introduced the fashion, short-lived as were all Macaroni innovations, of wearing iron heel clips so that they clinked with each step, although it seems unlikely that the noise could be heard above the general din.

The design of shoes does not take place in a vacuum. Changes in social environments have just as much influence as do fashion movements. Major upheavals like revolutions, or fundamental shifts in the nature of society, such as are caused by industrial advances, have their effects. But shoes are most susceptible to changes in sexual attitudes. They were altered by the French Revolution, as all of life was. The year 1789 was one of the great watersheds in the history of fashion. Eighteenth-century dress had generally been fairly static for men and women but, more than that, fashionable life was essentially urban, idle and privileged.

As the 1790s swept towards the nineteenth century on the wave of the Directoire, it became apparent that people's expectations were now different and that the balance between the sexes had changed. Women achieved a level of emancipation which made them look back in horror at the narrowly confined lives of their predecessors. Men no longer felt that serious subjects were the concern only of their fellow males. Nor did they consider an interest in clothes necessarily a sign of foppery. By the early nineteenth century, dandies like Beau Brummell had removed the sting of effeminacy from male pride in appearance. Far from being extravagantly extrovert in their dress, dandies were attracted by a rigorous simplicity. Not that life now was entirely without its affectations: the Beau let it be known that his man was allowed to clean his master's boots only with a mixture specially prepared from spent champagne and honey.

The nineteenth century was dominated by dancing. More than anything else, the craze for public balls affected attitudes to dress. Jane Austen's novels show the importance of balls in English social life, especially for the newly confident middle

Regency dandies. Detail from a 19th-century engraving

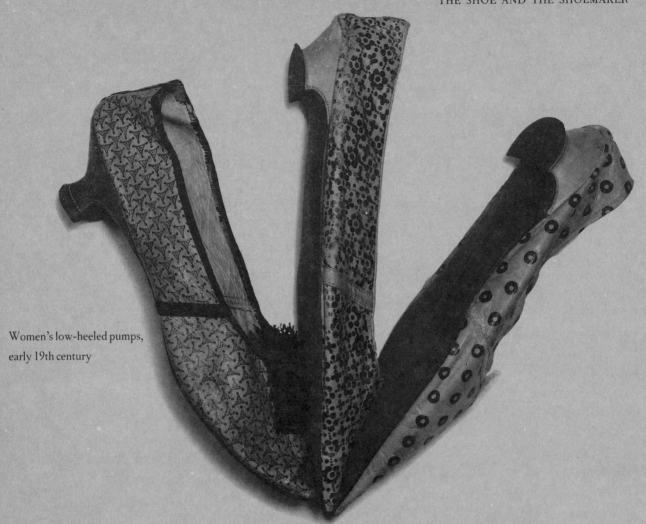

Women's low-heeled pumps,
early 19th century

Illustration from *Persuasion*, by
Jane Austen, 1987 edition

classes, and the same was true throughout Europe. The effect on footwear was soon apparent. Flat shoes came back into vogue, eventually doing away with 'straights', which could be worn on either foot and which had come in as a result of the development of the high heel. The first set of left and right lasts in the U.S. was developed by William Young of Philadelphia and was bought by Daniel Silsbee in 1822 for his production company.

The great craze of the dancing classes was the patent leather pump. The search for a leather with a permanently shiny surface had produced enamelled leather – shoe leather painted with linseed oil to produce a weatherproof gloss – but the final solution was found with the invention of patent leather in the 1790s. It became popular very quickly and was taken up by both sexes on each side of the Atlantic.

The plain, heel-less shoes worn by women in the first half of the nineteenth century achieved their look of extreme femininity by a simplicity of shape which, while appearing convincingly modern compared with eighteenth-century extravagance, managed also to seem vulnerable and delicate. When the style was extended up to the ankle to create little boots, both effects were even more pronounced.

By the middle of the century, heels had returned and the close-fitting, high-buttoned boot became the predominant fashion. J. Sparkes Hall, bootmaker to Queen Victoria, invented the elastic gusseted boot in 1837. It became a prominent style in the West and remained so, with variations, until the outset of World War I.

Almost equally as popular was the mid-century Balmoral boot, also designed by Sparkes Hall and closed by lacing. This had originally been created for Prince Albert, who liked it for its slenderizing effect, and such was his influence in England at the time that it became a great success with men, women and children.

The nineteenth century was as firmly the province of male footwear as the twentieth is of female footwear. Boot and shoe styles proliferated. Many were named after personalities. The lead in named boots was undoubtedly taken by military men, but one of the most elegant shoe styles was created by Count Alfred Guillaume Gabriel d'Orsay, perhaps the last of the French dandies.

Born in Paris in 1801, d'Orsay eventually entered the Garde du Corps. He met the Irish novelist and writer Lady Blessington in 1822 while stationed at Valence; they fell in love; he resigned his commission and travelled Europe with the Blessingtons before marrying Lord Blessington's daughter by a former wife. There was much scandal over his life with Lady Blessington, with whom d'Orsay finally took up residence after her husband's death. Despite a busy life as a man-about-town, author and artist, he found time in 1838 to design the d'Orsay pump, with cut-away sides and a V front. Originally a man's style, this has proved to be a perennial fashion shape, especially for women.

Not inappropriately for a century of wars, the nineteenth century was the era of the boot. Thanks to portrayals of John Bull, the top boot, worn with breeches, became the signature footwear of the British. An equally popular boot was the fashionable hessian, sometimes called the Austrian boot and named after the German state of Hesse. As the name suggests, it was originally a German fashion but it became smart footwear in fashionable cities throughout Europe. Introduced to England in the 1790s, it was a great favourite with Beau Brummell. Cut on a V at the front and decorated with a tassel, its appeal was a flamboyant one. As late as the 1870s Billy the Kid was still wearing boots based on the hessian.

Footwear introduced by military men proliferated. The Iron Duke, Arthur Wellesley, First Duke of Wellington, gave his name to the wellington boot. The original wellington was not of rubber, like the modern version, but of leather. Because it was of slim cut, it superseded the hessian as smart footwear for men-about-town. Having no tassel, it could be worn under the narrow cut trousers of the time without spoiling their line. A variation of the wellington, blocked in the same way and laced at the side, was the clarence, which was very popular in the nineteenth century. Named for the Duke of Clarence, it was castigated as the ugliest and most awkward of boots.

The Prince of Wahlstadt, Gebhard Leberecht von Blücher, a Prussian field-marshal, was second only to Wellington as a hero of the Battle of Waterloo. The blucher, a high-cut shoe with the tongue cut in one piece with the forepart and fastened with laces, was originally an army shoe but it has become a classic men's formal style, known today as a derby.

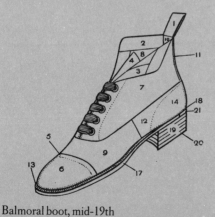

Balmoral boot, mid-19th century

Man's top boot (left) and wellington (right), 19th century

No matter how good a design might be, or what grand name is attached to it, a shoe is successful only if the shoemaker understands his craft. Shoes of any quality have only ever been produced by skilled shoemakers, although from earliest times in Europe (and in America in the eighteenth century) farmers had often used the long winter nights to make their own primitive shoes, for which the men cut the leather and the women bound the edge. Even as late as the nineteenth century, middle-class women made their own simple slippers for which patterns and embroidery suggestions were published. But for anything more durable they went to the shoemaker. Virtually every village had one. In *Our Village*, the English writer Mary Russell Mitford describes her local shoemaker. 'A pale, sickly-looking black-haired man', he was 'the very model of sober industry' and 'a man of substance; he employs three journeymen, two lame and one a dwarf, so that his shop looks like a hospital'.

Here Mrs Mitford sums up what were frequently the characteristics of the trade: industry, sobriety and ill-health. Because it was physically less demanding than much labouring work, families with a crippled or deformed son put him to be apprenticed to the craft of shoemaking. The work was sedentary and could be lucrative: Mrs Mitford's industrious shoemaker had purchased the lease of his 'commodious dwelling, some even say he has bought it out and out'. What she does not mention is the intellectual capacity and social awareness which have been exhibited by shoemakers throughout history. It was common practice for one of the members of the shop to spend part of the day reading the newspaper aloud while the others worked.

The first shoemakers were men, although Langland in the fourteenth-century poem *Piers Plowman* makes a distinction between Cesse (Cicely) the Soutresse and Clement the Cobbelere. They were apparently a musical crew. Dekker's Merry Cobbler of Ware 'did continually sing, so that this shop seemed a verrie birdcage'. In *The Cobbler of Canterburie*, written in 1590, the cobbler on his three-legged stool 'sung like a nightingale'.

These early shoemen were following the pattern set in ancient Greece, where shoemakers kept a crow which they taught to talk and sing in order to afford them company in their solitary working hours. In ancient Rome, the trade was more gregarious and shoemakers tended to cluster together in a particular street, just as in medieval London they were all found in the areas around the Royal Exchange and St Martin le Grand.

The craft of shoemaking is an ancient one and its early history is shrouded in legend. The patron saint of shoemakers is St Crispin and his story has come down to us in various forms. In the French legend, Crispin and his twin brother Crispianus left Rome to escape the wrath of the Emperor Diocletian. They arrived in Soissons where they were pursued by Maximus, who was under orders from the Emperor to destroy them. Maximus tried to drown them; he plunged them into boiling oil; he smothered them in white-hot lead, but he failed to kill them. Finally, he took the easy way out and beheaded them. The legend has two versions from this point. In one, the bodies were sent to England and were lost in a shipwreck off the coast of Kent. In the other, the brothers' bones were divided between two churches in Northern France where the sick could make a pilgrimage, touch the bones and be cured.

The English version of the legend is more romantic but no more convincing. It is centered on Kent, where the two brothers, sons of the Queen of Kent, were

St Crispin and his brother, patron saints of shoemakers

again menaced by Maximus. Disguised as poor peasants they fled Canterbury, their native town, and hid in Faversham. Crispin became bound apprentice to a shoemaker. His master sent him to Canterbury with shoes for the Emperor's daughter, Ursula. He fell in love with her and they secretly married. Crispianus, who had become a soldier in the Roman army, had honours piled on him by Maximus who, discovering that both brothers were of noble birth, became reconciled to the secret marriage, which was openly confirmed on 25 October – the traditional shoemakers' holiday.

A more tragic shoemaking legend is that of Hugh of Wales. The son of a Welsh king, Hugh fell in love with Winifred, whose father was king of another part of Wales. She rejected him in favour of the religious life and Hugh, after much wandering, became a shoemaker. Later, he and Winifred were both executed by Diocletian. She was bled to death and he was hanged. His bones were stolen from the gibbet by fellow shoemakers who made them into tools. This is why the term 'St Hugh's bones' is the traditional name for shoemakers' tools.

Shoemaking has for centuries been known as 'the gentle craft', an expression first found in the sixteenth-century play 'George-a'-Green'. In it, Edward IV, who has been walking around London in disguise, falls in with some shoemakers. They treat him kindly and offer him hospitality. To show his gratitude, the King removes his disguise and gives them a toast: 'because you have drunk with the King . . . you and yours to the world's end shall be called the trade of the gentle craft'.

Like all medieval craftsmen, shoemakers founded their own guilds. One of the earliest was in England. It was called the Guild of Cordwainers, a name taken from a corruption of Cordova, the town in Spain from which the best leather (cordovan) came in the Middle Ages. Like other guilds at this time, its main role was to ensure that standards of workmanship were set and maintained. The London Cordwainers, whose motto was 'corio et arte', issued its first Ordinance in 1272 and gave its first fine through Gregory de Ramesay, one of the Guild wardens, who charged John Joy 40 pence in 1345 for using inferior leather for his shoes.

To become a shoemaker, a man had to serve a seven-year apprenticeship, after which he was declared a masterman, although before receiving his titles he had to prove his skill by producing a masterpiece. Many shoemakers lived at a level of considerable grandeur. John Peachey, famous in the reign of James V and known as 'the shoemaker of Fleet Street', employed more than forty men, not including apprentices, and dressed them in his own special livery. They accompanied him to church and each one had a sword and buckler. Shoemakers often became very rich. When John Cams of Cheapside died in 1796, he left £37,000 to charity.

Guilds sprang up around Europe: Holland's first guild was founded in Ghent in 1304 and the Confrère des Compagnons Cordonniers de Paris was registered in 1379. The cordwainers' guilds were prominent in public affairs. In the Chester Mystery plays, the cordwainers represented Christ's Entry into Jerusalem. The same guild was ordered to provide a ball of leather every Shrove Tuesday for the citizens of the town to use as a football. The London Cordwainers, along with other guilds, provided Whifflers – 'terrible, monstrous men' – to clear the Lord Mayor's path on ceremonial occasions.

Shoemakers were frequently non-conformists and often Quakers – in fact, the movement's founder George Fox had been apprenticed to a shoemaker in Leicestershire, England. Because of their religious principles, many shoemakers found themselves in trouble during the seventeenth century. Philip Kirkland and

St Crispin fitting a shoe on Princess Ursula, from a copy of *The History of the Gentle Craft*, 1676 edition

Arms of the London Cordwainers

Henry Elwell, from Buckinghamshire, fleeing from religious persecution, settled in Lynn, Massachusetts, in 1635, and set up their own establishment. They were not the first immigrant shoemakers to arrive in America. Christopher Nelme had left Bristol on the *Margaret* and arrived in Virginia in September 1619.

The shoemakers from the Old World who settled in the New were quick to learn how to make moccasins based on the buckskin originals of the American Indians. By the middle of the seventeenth century the colonists were exporting moccasins in considerable numbers to England, where they had a brief, but intense, vogue. The question of protective tariffs had long exercised shoemakers' guilds in Europe and England, and it was not long before it became a problem for the shoemakers in America. At the First Congress, held in Philadelphia in the winter of 1789, it was decided to impose a tariff on imported footwear: 50 cents per pair for boots and 7 cents for shoes. The measure was piloted through Congress by Roger Sharman, a former shoemaker who had been one of the signatories of the Declaration of Independence.

Vast quantities of shoes and boots were required as the industrial revolution began to take effect. Although mass-production grew at an enormous rate in the nineteenth century, it was not new. As early as the sixteenth century, London shoemakers had been employing as many as sixty journeymen to turn out shoes in large numbers. Ready-to-wear shoes were brought a stage nearer in Norwich, England, around 1792, when John Smith abandoned the practice of measuring every foot and began to make boots of different sizes which could be tried on and bought on the spot. Two years later in America, Quincy and Harvey Reed, who had previously sold boots from a horse-drawn carriage, opened the country's first retail boot store in Boston, where they displayed shoes and boots on Wednesdays and Saturdays. By 1800, New England was the centre of the Ten Foot Shoe Shop, a name given to small wooden shacks which littered the countryside. Called ten footers because of their size, they were situated in the backyards of farms, and sold ready-made shoes direct from a master shoemaker, who usually had two journeymen and an apprentice working for him.

The American shoe trade moved forward quickly and, by the 1850s, was leaving Europe trailing. Part of the reason for this was the speed with which the Americans assimilated new mechanical advances. Also, scarcity of labour in America encouraged mass-production, with the result that despite higher costs American manufacturers could produce a wider range of styles at more competitive prices than European manufacturers. Considerable quantities of cheap, well-made American shoes were exported to England, causing a crisis in the British boot trade. By 1901, more than one million pairs of American shoes were being imported annually and British manufacturers were forced to take up the new production methods to counter the flood.

Although the U.S. was not entirely free of strikes, the unrest caused by industrial innovation in the American trade was not so great as in England. In 1858, Lyman R. Blake of Abingdon, Massachusetts, invented a machine for sewing the soles of shoes, replacing the hand-sewing that had been in use since Roman times. A shortage of skilled workers in the U.S. had forced manufacturers to attach the soles with pegs. The Blake patents were developed by Gordon McKay, who substituted thread for the heavy and cumbersome nails and pegs. Women workers in Lynn, Massachusetts, were quick to realize that this advance would eventually endanger their jobs and, in 1859, they called the first general strike in the trade –

sixty-three years after the earliest labour strike in the United States, which had been staged in Philadelphia by shoemakers demanding more money.

As in all other fields in the nineteenth century, industrialization could not be held back. Inventions were changing the shoe industry from a craft-based trade to a mechanized one. By 1864, the improved Blake sewer was available commercially in the U.S. and England. Using this machine, competent machinists could sew up to three dozen pairs of shoes per hour – a production rate unimaginable ten years previously. The speed of sewing was the key to increased production, and inventions which offered any improvement were eagerly taken up, especially by the American industry. Twelve years before Blake's invention, Elias Howe of Massachusetts had assigned the British rights of his lock-stitch sewing machine to William Thomas of London. Ten years later, Thomas's sewing machines – or similar types – marketed by the Singer Company of New York were in general use throughout the trade. The ancient craft of handmade shoe production was about to be superseded.

In its place came a virile new industry which was able to produce fashionable and comfortable shoes in vast quantities and at prices which made them accessible to a wider range of people than before. As the twentieth century began, the shoe industry faced a confident future. Of course, the old handcrafted methods of shoemaking were not cast off immediately. The quality end of the business was still a hand-based trade. Mass-manufactured shoes were aimed almost entirely at the lower-middle and working classes. The 'carriage trade' still patronized the bootmakers. At the upper end of the market, the dominant influence was male. It was considered that everything could be known of a man by the shoes he wore and infinite pains were taken by shoemaker and client to make sure that they correctly reflected his status.

Lesley Lewis's *The Private Life of a Country House* (1980) gives us an insight into the importance attached to a gentleman's shoes as late as the 1920s. Lewis vividly recalls the boots and shoes worn by her father and the almost ritualistic treatment they received:

He had a boot cupboard containing about 20 pairs of boots and shoes, all most beautifully made for him by a firm called Taylor. There were black boots with grey cloth tops for formal wear; leather ones for everyday; several pairs of brown shoes of varying weights for country wear; shooting boots – greased instead of polished; white buckskin tennis shoes with rubber soles; and patent-leather pumps for evening dress, with low fronts and little black bows. As time went on, he gave up boots except for shooting but always kept in his room an old pair of gloves to use when putting on and lacing up footwear. Unlike our more ordinary shoes, which were polished by the houseboy with Kiwi or Cherry Blossom in an outside boot hole, my father's were done in the pantry by the butler, with browning or blacking from an earthenware bottle. The syrupy liquid was applied with a stick and then rubbed in and burnished with a stag- or beef-bone to produce a deep gloss which, considering all the work that went into it, was surprisingly vulnerable. Puppies had to be taught very early not to lick it . . . it contained some ingredient to which they could become addicted.

It is noteworthy that Lewis dismisses her mother's shoes as being 'by the firm that made my father's' and gives no details of their style or treatment. In fact, it was quite common, certainly as late as the 1940s, for women who could afford bespoke shoes to have them made by a bootmaker in the men's trade. The great shoemakers of London, for example, such as Lobb and McAfee, made women's shoes rather on the side, as they still do. The bulk of their trade is in making shoes for men. Of course, there were specialist bespoke shoemakers for women and several of them became world famous. Perugia, David Evins and Ferragamo all built their reputations on 'one-offs' for fashionable women.

The bespoke shoemakers have kept alive the traditional skills. Shoes are individually made today using the same techniques as those used two hundred years ago. Everything is done by hand – from the making of the beech last, using an outline of the foot and a line which traces the inner line of the arch, to the final polishing and preparation of the shoe before it is presented to the customer. The process is time-consuming. In handcrafted work corners cannot be cut. It is not surprising that shoemen talk of 'building' a shoe. However, the customer is usually happy to wait – and to pay the large price which is necessary in order to have his individual last and uniquely made shoe.

Bespoke shoemakers are now found only in the most fashionable of cities. Despite the frequently expressed opinion that they are an anachronism, the few firms that have survived the dramatic reduction in the numbers of bespoke shoemen do very well, whether they are in Rome, Boston or Vienna. The best known bespoke shoemakers in the world are probably Lobb of St James's in London. They have traditionally supplied footwear to the English aristocracy and the European nobility – which is why Lobb opened a branch in Paris in 1901 – but since the 1920s the American market has played an increasingly important role in sales and now accounts, along with film and pop stars, for a considerable percentage of the turnover in bespoke work in London.

It seems that when men reach a peak in their careers, they turn from ready-to-wear to bespoke shoes. The order books of Lobb and McAfee are a roll call of this century's achievers. Lobb have always made shoes for male members of the British Royal Family, but their customers come from every walk of life. They include actors and theatre men, such as Clifton Webb and Cole Porter; a wide range of writers from Somerset Maugham to Leslie Charteris; and world figures like Marconi. The customer list at McAfee contains a high percentage of entertainers and showbusiness personalities. Fred Astaire, Cary Grant, Laurel and Hardy, James Stewart, John Ford, Sam Goldwyn, Henry Mancini . . . it is a checklist of Hollywood's 'greats'. In addition, King Constantine and the Princess of Wales both buy McAfee shoes 'off the peg' – the latter, specifically for Prince Charles.

Manolo Blahnik, photograph by Michael Roberts, 1989

# THE SHOEMAKER'S ART

A shoemaker knows things about his client's feet that it might be better to keep the world ignorant of. Every bump and blemish must be taken into account if a handmade shoe is to fit perfectly. Once made, the shoe can only be correctly fitted if the shoemaker handles the foot that is to wear it. The sexual implications are obvious and, in the past, the opportunities for illicit dalliance at the shoemaker's provided a rich, and probably not entirely unjustified, vein for satirists and moralists. Behind the fantasy, the reality was mundane enough. Shoemakers were normally kept in their place and worked long hours for small profits. Their craftsmanship was frequently exquisite but their lives were far removed from the gilded world of the fashionable courts.

In the twentieth century, mass-manufacture has reached such a high

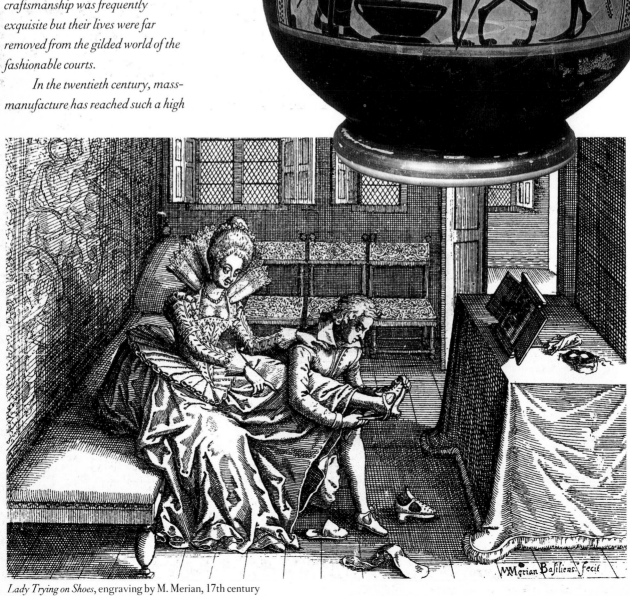

*Lady Trying on Shoes*, engraving by M. Merian, 17th century

42

level of sophistication that comfort and fit have never been better and the variety of choice available to all members of the public has never been greater. The most pampered eighteenth-century courtesan would be amazed by the range of styles on sale today. In her time design was a matter of consultation between client and shoemaker. Off-the-peg fashion shoes did not exist, although itinerant shoemakers sold ready-made boots to peasant workmen for whom fit was not considered so important and style was not even a consideration.

*Opposite:* Greek vase painting showing shoemaker making shoes to measure, *c.* 500 BC

*Right:* Etching by unknown French artist, late 17th century

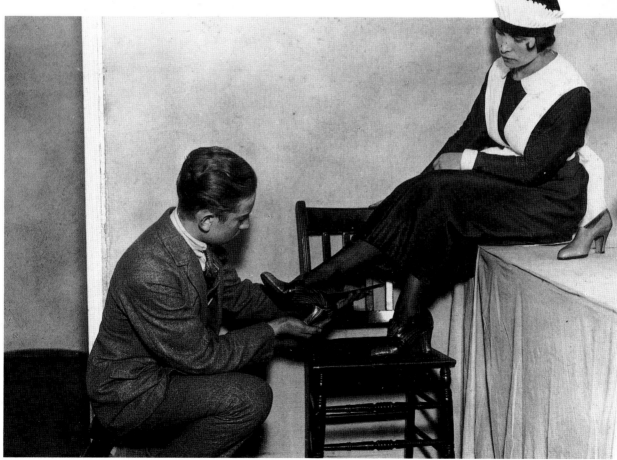

Scene at an International Shoe and Leather Fair in the 1920s

# TRADITIONAL SKILLS

The basic skills of shoemaking have barely changed since earliest times. The shoemaker portrayed in this Roman relief would feel perfectly at home in the reconstruction of a cobbler's shop in Northampton Museum, England. He would be able to pick up the tools with the confidence of complete familiarity. He would also understand the functions of the shoemaker's equipment displayed in the engraving published in Germany in 1750. This rather fancy-dress character has leather-cutting knives and files decorating his hat; a variety of awls tucked into his cuff; pincers tied to his boots; a tape measure and wooden lasts slung around his neck and a shoe measure in his right hand. All are still in use in bespoke shoemaking today.

In the middle of the last century, shoemaking, in common with most other crafts, moved from the craftsman's shop to the factory floor. In order that full advantage might be taken of the advances in equipment, skilled workers were grouped together under one roof, as they are in this picture of the Manfield factory in the 1900s.

Many modern young shoemakers have returned to production methods which use a high proportion of handwork. Christine Ahrens is typical of these.

*Top:* Roman relief showing shoemaker at work

*Above:* Reconstruction of a cobbler's shop, Northampton Museum, England

*Right:* Etching of a shoemaker, by C. Horman, before 1750

*Opposite:* Closing room at the Manfield shoe factory, Northampton, England, c. 1900

*Opposite inset:* Shoe designer Christine Ahrens, 1989

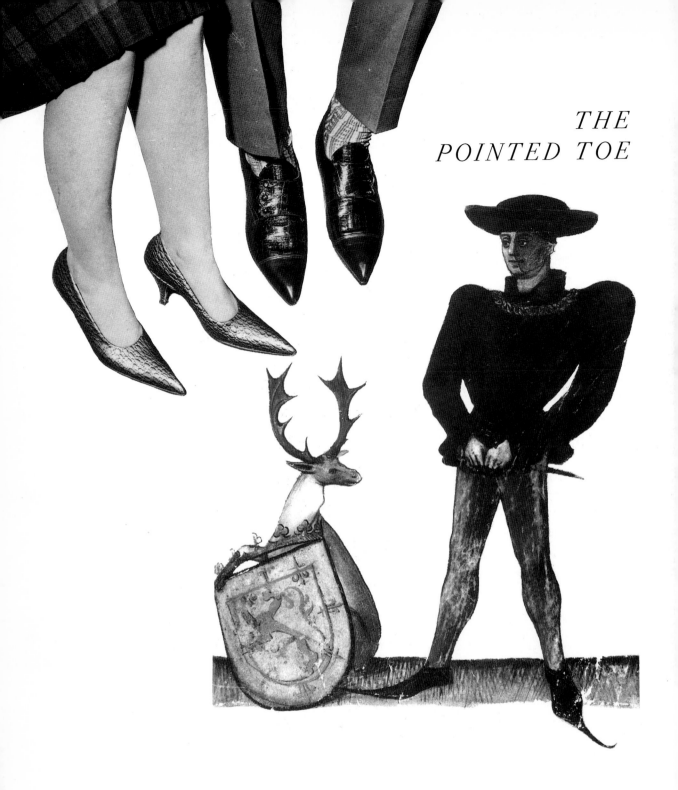

# THE POINTED TOE

*Top:* Winkle-pickers, 1960

*Above:* Portrait of James II of Scotland (1430-60), illumination by Jörg von Ehingen

Exaggeration is a constant theme of fashion. It is employed to give maximum impact to a new look and to prolong the life of a dying one.

The evolution of shoe styles is much slower than the changes in other items of clothing so the use of exaggeration to make a new fashion statement is rarely necessary. The elongated toe, which made its first appearance in the twelfth century, was one of the first examples of a comparatively sudden fashion change in footwear. It did not evolve as the result of a new technique and was not a response to a recently emerged need. It was a true fashion change in that it was conceived as something to make other styles seem déclassé. The long pointed-toed shoe, known as the poulaine or crackowe, was a dandy fashion. It was totally urban, as all fashion must initially be, and was confined to the courts and capitals of Europe. Its impracticality for normal everyday wear proclaimed its wearer to be a man of privilege.

46

*Bishops and other guardians of public morality lost no time in railing against the poulaine as a piece of gross licentiousness. They were right to do so. The poulaine had much the same effect as the codpiece a couple of centuries later: it glorified masculine sexuality in a most obvious way. Edicts banning the wearing of poulaines or attempting to regulate the length of the toe were largely ignored. The fashion was ousted only when a new fad – the broad-toed shoe – took its place.*

*The poulaine was largely forgotten until this century – at least as a fashion source. In the 1960s, pointed toes and narrow uppers became stylish with the young and liberated. Winkle-pickers are largely associated with sharp young men but they were also worn by girls. In fact, women's shoes with pointed toes and stiletto heels had a much longer fashion life than the male version. Paco Rabanne resurrected poulaines in 1984 but they were little more than fancy dress.*

*Top:* Poulaines with pattens, known as 'devils' claws', *c.* 1440

*Above:* From the collection of Paco Rabanne, Summer 1984

# THE CHOPINE

Chopines were possibly the most theatrical and artificial style of footwear ever conceived. They originated in the East, where they were worn for hygienic reasons by women visiting the public baths; the cothurni *worn by Greek actors to increase their stature and give dignity to their movements had the same high soles, but these shoes really came into their own in their most exaggerated form in sixteenth-century Venice. They were talked about in European court circles; they were mentioned in Hamlet and, predictably enough, condemned by the church (the Archpriest of Talavera in Spain felt obliged in 1438 to castigate the 'depraved and dissolute women' who wore painted chopines).*

*Like all extreme fashion at this time and for centuries to come, the use of chopines could only have been contemplated by the privileged who lived lives of idleness: no working woman could hope to wear them and be able to carry out her duties. Surprisingly, if they ever achieved a 'height of fashion' status outside Venice, few women chose to have their portraits painted wearing chopines. In fact, it seems likely that this shoe was one of the earliest recorded fashion fads, doomed to be talked of and laughed at but worn by only the most crazed followers of fashion, rather like hot pants in our own time. Chopines were worn as business shoes by Venetian prostitutes who used the height and statuesque demeanour they provided in order to make themselves visible.*

*Above: Two Courtesans* by Vittore Carpaccio, *c.* 1500

*Right:* Italian chopines, wood, covered with cut and
punched white leather, early 17th century

*Opposite left:* Venetian courtesan, etching from the 'Diversarium
Nationum Ornatus des Alexander Fabri', 1593

*Opposite right:* Ivory statuette of a Greek actor wearing *cothurni*

# THE SPIRIT
# OF THE AGE

All art forms reflect the thoughts of their time. None are created in a
vacuum. They interact to produce a spirit of the age which manifests itself
with remarkable similarity across various creative fields. Visually, there is
frequently a considerable conformity of thought between architects and
clothes makers concerning shape, scale and proportion.

The peak-toed poulaine of the fourteenth and fifteenth centuries and
the wide-toed shoe that followed it display striking similarities to the
architecture of their periods just as Perugia's aerodynamic heel of steel alloy
can be seen to embody something of the spirit of the new age of engineering
exemplified by the Brooklyn Bridge.

*Above left:* Perugia evening sandal with rhinestone-paved strips of gold-plated steel
alloy, 1953

*Above right:* Brooklyn Bridge, built by John and Washington Roebling, 1867-82

*Right:* Leather poulaine with side lacing, before 1420

*Far right:* Salisbury Cathedral, Wiltshire, England, 1220-60, with 14th-century spire

*Opposite:* Nave vault, Sherborne Abbey, Dorset, England, 1475-1504

*Inset:* King Henry VIII, after 1537, from an original by Holbein

50

*Venus and Adonis* by
Janssens van Nuyssen
(d. 1632)

*Right:* Fragment from a
bronze equestrian statue, Roman,
1st Century AD, showing *caliga*

# SANDALS

Few items of clothing emit as many different messages as sandals do. They range from the fuddy-duddy and dull to the glamorous and free. Above all, sandals are the simplest and most direct practical response to the need to protect the feet. In fact, they were the earliest form of wrought foot covering.

Sandals were the basic footwear of all Mediterranean cultures. There is little variation between Egyptian and Etruscan sandals; those of Greece and Rome are almost identical. Their openness and simplicity made them ideal for warm climates but, as they moved northwards and were more enclosed, they became the precursors of the modern boot.

The straps and thongs of the early sandal served a dual purpose. In addition to giving support and strength to the ankle when the wearer was crossing rough terrain, they were also, in the Roman army, an indication of his rank. When they extended above the ankle, the sandal was the footwear of an officer. Called calige, these sandals were often studded with gold and silver. Gaius Caesar, Roman emperor from 37 to 41 AD, wore his calige so regularly that his soldiers called him Caligula. European painters constantly reinvented the caliga in fanciful forms, as Piero di Cosima and Janssens van Nuyssen have done in the two paintings shown here.

Detail from *Death of Procris* by Piero di Cosimo, *c.* 1515

# SANDAL PLAY

Right: Sandals shown with the Per Spook Collection, Spring/Summer 1986

*Below:* Sandals by Patrick Cox, 1987

*Women wearing styles more normally associated with children, like this simple buckled sandal, can look as perversely alluring as little girls who clump around in mother's high-heeled slippers.*

*Men in sandals give out very different signals. All military associations are gone (no one could imagine this young man as a centurion) and, in their stead, we have connotations of a healthy unworldliness. This adult version of the schoolboy sandal derives its chic from being decked out in the two-toned trappings of the glamorous spectator shoe of the 1930s. An additional frisson is afforded the fashionably aware by recognition of the fact that the two-toned effect is identical to that in Chanel's famous sling-back sandal for women.*

*Opposite page*
*Top:* Sandal manufactured by Dolcis, 1954

*Far right:* Sandals, 1934, photographed by Steichen for French *Vogue*

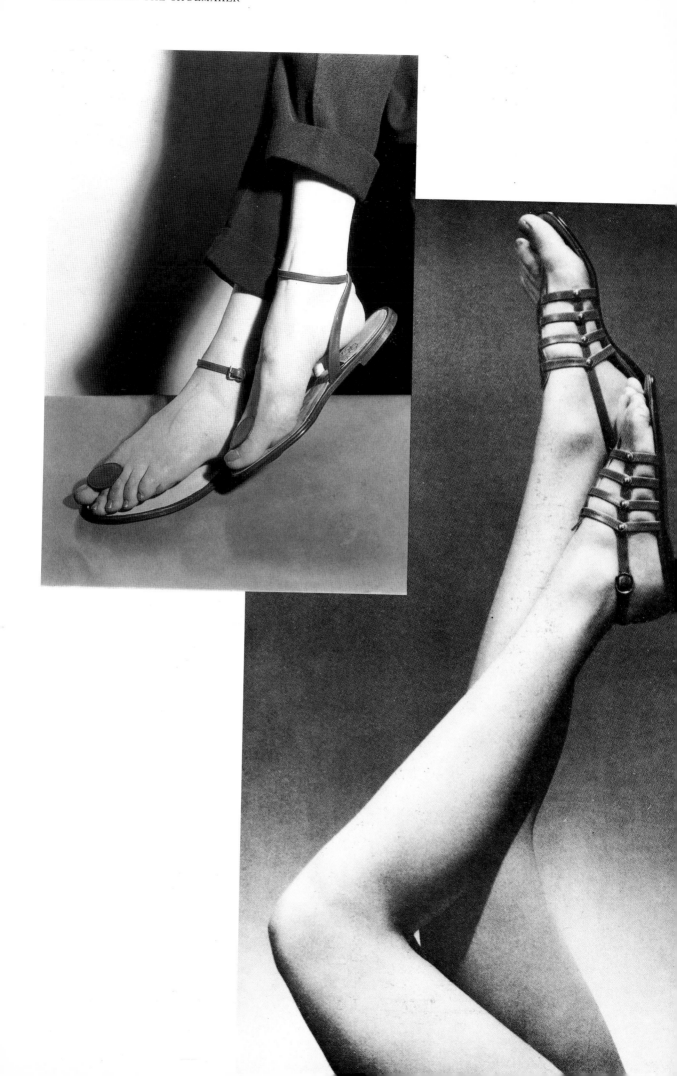

# SO THAT THE WIND

would not blow him away, Philetas of Cos, who died in 290 BC, wore lead-soled sandals. Julius Caesar is reputed to have worn boots with golden soles for ceremonial occasions. Nero, who frequently wore silver-soled sandals, is supposed to have been wearing special gold-soled sandals on the day he killed his wife Poppaea by kicking her to death. Heliogabalus is recorded as never wearing a pair of shoes more than once.

Whether or not they are apocryphal, there are enough tales about the shoes of the ancients to show that the nobility considered fine footwear a privilege and a luxury. Rulers and generals were not alone in wearing high-quality status sandals; philosophers and prostitutes wore them too. There is some evidence to suggest that 'designer' shoes were commissioned by the high born as burial shoes which would enable them to walk proudly in the next world.

The sandal was the commonest Roman style. Of chased leather, frequently embellished with gold and silver and even, on occasion, studded with jewels and semi-precious stones, it was an attention-seeking object. Much thought was given both to its ornamentation and to the arrangement of the nails on the sole, which made a distinctive pattern on the ground. Like their counterparts in Greece, Roman

Detail from *Mars Disarmed by Venus and The Three Graces* by Jacques-Louis David, 1824

*Top:* Silver sandal from an Egyptian tomb, Byzantine, 6th century AD

*Above:* Treading one's enemy underfoot. From an Egyptian sandal

courtesans left footprints in the sand which read, 'Follow me'. Every Roman legion had its unique nail pattern, and the crack regiments of Antiochus' army were reputed to have nails made of gold. Greek and Roman soldiers were so conscious of their appearance that they were often warned against becoming too obsessed. The Greek historian Polybius records that soldiers had to be specifically cautioned against devoting too much thought to their sandals at the expense of the rest of their equipment. Emperors dressed to highlight their difference from their subjects and to emphasize their strength. Like the Gods, whom they attempted to emulate, they were beautifully shod, usually in distinctive white footwear made of leather lightened by being steeped in alum. Because the lightening process was slow and costly, pale-coloured sandals became a mark of wealth and position. In fact, any form of footwear was a sign of some status since slaves and the poorer classes went barefoot.

As in the later courts of Europe, fashions in the ancient world were frequently initiated to gratify a royal need for exclusivity, though they were nearly always taken up by the aristocracy and then copied by the middle classes. In Sumeria, for example, shoes with turned up points were originally permitted only to kings and princes but were later made obligatory for anyone attending formal court ceremonies. Eventually they became commonplace throughout Syria, where they are still worn today.

Although priests occupied an important position in ancient societies, they almost invariably performed their offices barefoot as an outward and visible sign of their inward humility and purity. Their sandals for outdoor wear were simple and undecorated to signify the priestly disregard for comfort and worldly luxury – and they have remained so for those reasons into modern times. The clergy in the Middle Ages performed their religious ceremonies in simple leather sandals of rustic and archaic design to symbolize their separation from worldly vanities.

Footwear has a significance and a role beyond merely clothing the feet. In the Middle Ages, it was common for princes to present sandals to the Pope as a sign of solidarity between State and Church. The symbolism surrounding shoes goes back to ancient Egypt, where contempt and loathing of one's enemy was signified by painting a representation of him on the sole of one's sandal. In Greece, a sole painting of the image of a loved one had exactly the opposite symbolic meaning.

Shoes have traditionally been used to symbolize a person's rights. The Law of Moses stated that if a man did not wish to marry his brother's widow, she could take him to court and publicly proclaim the fact by removing his shoe and denouncing him with the words, 'So shall it be done unto that man who will not build up his brother's house.' As a form of curse, its power derived from the fact that the shoe was a symbol of security and prosperity. The giving of a shoe to reinforce a contract and symbolize a bond is mentioned in the Book of Ruth: 'for to confirm all things, a man plucked off his shoe and gave it to his neighbour and this was taken as testimony in Israel.'

Shoes were also emblems of temporal power. As the Middle Ages waned, courtly extravagance increased. Clothing was used as a status symbol; kings were elaborately shod. On ceremonial occasions, Charlemagne appeared in jewel-encrusted boots and his son, Louis the Debonaire, wore boots of gold. Bernard, King of Italy, was buried in magnificent red leather boots. There was a predictable reaction against such extravagance: from his pulpit Guillaume of Dijon denounced what he considered indecent footwear betokening vanity.

Such invective had little effect and costly garb continued to be part of the panoply of kingship. The Plantagenets introduced a degree of style into England, though the English lacked the grandiosity of their French rivals. They looked at their most impressive in their death effigies. Henry II is wearing green leather boots ornamented in gold; Richard I's boots are also gold decorated and Edward III, during whose reign the level of court luxury reached heights that were considered by the Church to be scandalous, is depicted in his effigy in Westminster Abbey wearing splendidly embroidered boots.

The determination to look magnificent was accompanied by an equal conviction that such magnificence must be reserved to royalty. Commoners were not allowed to dress on the same level of luxury. Sumptuary laws to impose the details of apparel which each class might wear continued through the sixteenth century, but attempts to deny such a basic pleasure as the joy in finery could never hope for much success. In fact, like Prohibition in the United States, they were at best a holding operation and at worst liable to weaken authority by exposing its impotence. Not that sumptuary laws were confined to modern centuries. In ancient Rome, only those who had served in the office of Edile were allowed to wear red; the Emperor Aurelius forbad men to wear coloured shoes and Heliogabalus would not allow women to ornament their shoes with gold or precious stones.

Authority's determination to take a stand often indicates fear, and nothing alarmed the authorities throughout Europe more than the spread of the poulaine. There was a flurry of edicts to try to stamp it out. All the concerted efforts of Church and State failed and it ran its course until it was overtaken by a new fashion. Pope Urban V spoke out against poulaines. Charles V of France banned his personal secretaries and notaries from wearing them and, in 1368, warned 'all persons of any quality' to abandon the style 'on pain of being mulcted in a penalty of 34 francs from using in future long peaked shoes'.

No fashion has caused so much fuss. The disapproval rumbled across Europe. Edward IV of England published sumptuary decrees to try to stop poulaines being made and worn. One statute informed shoemakers that if they made for 'unprivileged' persons any boots or shoes with toes exceeding 2 inches in length they would be forfeit twenty shillings, 'one noble to be paid to the king, another to the Cordwainers of London, and another to the Chamber of London'. Edward's statute of 1463 stated that 'no knight under the state of Lord . . . shall use or wear . . . any shoes or boots having spikes passing the length of two inches upon pain to forfeit to the king, for every default, 3 shillings and 4 pence'.

As late as 1639, Massachusetts' General Court made a public proclamation denouncing the 'common' classes for attempting through dress 'to rise above their designated position in society', and twelve years later the Massachusetts colonial legislature pronounced its 'utter detestation' that the lowly 'should take on the badges of gentlemen by wearing . . . boots with roses affixed'.

To maintain magnificent attire requires great dedication and considerable sums of money. Kings and aristocrats paid up because the results were as awe-inspiring as the bills. One of the most interesting aspects of old account books is the number of shoes and boots that a man of public importance required to get him through the annual round of court appearances, commercial dealings, country pursuits and dalliance. In England in Tudor times, Lord Lisle ordered 20 pairs of quarter shoes, 2 pairs of boots, 2 pairs of buckskins and 5 pairs of Spanish leather shoes in nineteen months. If Hamlet's complaint that his mother had married too soon is typical – 'A little month, or ere those shoes were old, with which she followed my poor father's body' – sixteenth-century shoes had a very limited life. Costs continued to rise. Between 1633 and 1635, Charles I paid his shoemaker £54.13.10 'for 90 pairs of shooes; 27 pairs of Thinn Bootes; 2 pairs of Spanish leather Bootes; 6 pairs of Strong Thicke Bootes; 2 pairs of slippers and for Sattin for one paire of them'.

It is no wonder that beautiful shoes and handsome boots figured in fairytales and superstitions. Votive shoes in clay have survived from Roman times and early bronze and silver shoes have been found in tombs in Syria, Greece and a majority of the Mediterranean countries. All attest to the power of the shoe as a symbol. The message of tomb shoes is clear enough: they were there to ensure that the deceased walked in splendour in the otherworld. The practice of burying a pair of shoes with the dead survives in certain parts of the world. Other superstitions are even more persistent and none appears more frequently in all cultures than the shoe or boot as a symbol of luck. It was because it was seen as a bringer of good fortune that early drinking vessels were often in the shape of a boot, to signify a free-flowing plenty. Amulets to ward off dangers and devils were frequently in the shape of shoes.

Even in the twentieth century, playground games keep alive the idea of shoes bringing luck. A child with new shoes will have them trodden on 'for luck', or if a child sees a white horse he will mark the sole of his shoe with the sign of the cross and say, 'White horse, white horse; bring me luck, today or tomorrow.' In virtually all European cultures it is considered very bad luck to put new shoes on a table because of the association with the laying out of a corpse, wearing its best shoes. It is well known that should new shoes creak as a person walks along, they have not been paid for.

Shoes were given as love tokens by young men to symbolize their desire to share their worldly goods with the girl of their choice. This practice was normally restricted to the peasant classes, but it came into polite society in the eighteenth century when it became the rage to exchange elegant porcelain models of shoes. In England in 1791 a lifesize print was published of the Duchess of York's shoe, which was only 5¾ inches long and 1¾ inches wide. This started a craze for porcelain representations of shoes.

Sentimental Victorians exchanged miniature shoes in leather, pottery, treen, alabaster, silver and brass. Wooden snuff boxes shaped like a shoe were also

The Duchess of York's shoe, lifesize, 1790s

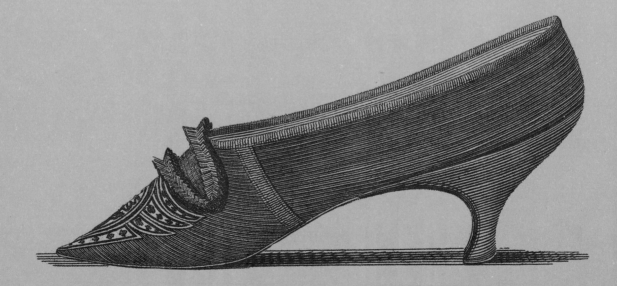

popular. In all cases, the shoe was associated with the hope of a contented, settled and prosperous life. Slightly less sentimental Victorians carried gin flasks in the shape of women's boots and paper knives in the shape of high-heeled shoes!

In courtship and marriage, the desire for luck and prosperity is linked with the hope of fecundity. Superstition and shoes were involved in all three hopes. It began with the search for a husband: in Norfolk, England, girls put a clover leaf in their shoes in the belief that they would marrry the next single man they met. This was an extremely common superstition, as was the belief that if a girl's shoe came undone, her future lover was thinking of her.

At the marriage ceremony, fathers gave their daughter's shoes to the groom to symbolize that her well-being was now his responsibility and, in some countries, the groom would tap the bride lightly on the head with her shoe to prove that he was the master. As recently as the 1940s in the Veneto, Northern Italy, a ritual parallel with the Cinderella story still took place as part of wedding ceremonies. The family and guests would attempt to fit a shoe on the bride's foot, but the only one able to succeed would be the groom.

In Finland a young couple are traditionally accompanied to their bedroom by the entire wedding party. The bride's mother will not allow the new husband to go to bed until he has given her a pair of shoes. In other countries the bride's wedding shoe is placed at the head of the bed on the husband's side to symbolize his sexual possession and to encourage fertility. There is a tradition in Germany that a pregnant woman wear her husband's shoes, the idea being that as the husband is stronger, the wife may gain strength by wearing them.

Such folk customs have largely died out, though throwing an old boot after a newly wed couple, or tying it to the vehicle taking them from the church, survives as a way of wishing them luck. However, links with the past still exist in fairy stories which originated as folk tales and were part of the verbal tradition of most Western cultures. The best known of these is probably Cinderella, of which there are more than three hundred versions.

The Cinderella story was already old when it was first written down in China during the 9th century AD. The European version is by Charles Perrault, who published it in France in his *Tales of Mother Goose* of 1697. In it, he changed two of the components of the original folk versions. He substituted a fairy godmother for a friendly beast and a glass slipper for one of fur.

The idea of the protective beast, usually a domestic animal, able to communicate with humans, is common in fairytales. It is part of the supernatural element necessary to many of them. In Cinderella, if we take the orphan's benefactor to be an animal, for example a cat, then the shoe of fur becomes much more closely linked with the provider of it. Domestic animals are cuddly and warm; so are fur shoes. Such shoes have an obvious sexual connotation, but it is totally removed if glass is substituted. Psychiatrists have pointed out that the hearth where Cinderella was forced to remain by her step-mother and sisters is the traditionally recognized position for a youngest child, representing the warmth and privilege of maternal love. A domestic animal and fur shoe enhance the feeling of warmth.

Boots, also, are important in Perrault's tales, not only in the story of Puss in Boots – aptly described as the Figaro of the nursery – but also in 'Hop o' My Thumb', in which seven-league boots play a crucial role. In this tale, abandoned children wander through a wood until they come to an ogre's castle. Entertained by his wife, they hide when the ogre returns. He smells their human flesh and

The Master Cat, or: Puss-in-Boots, from *Fairy Tales* by Charles Perrault

determines to eat them. Hop o' My Thumb places the golden crowns of the ogre's own children on the heads of his brothers and, feeling for them in the dark, the ogre is fooled into eating his own family. He pursues the boys in his seven-league boots but they are saved when Thom steals the boots and thereby robs him of his power. The idea that footwear, like any other type of clothes, can change an individual and make him seem tyrannical is common enough. What the Perrault tale is saying is that once divested of symbols of power, individuals are no longer able to inspire fear.

Hans Christian Andersen's 'The Red Shoes' is a tale of vanity punished. The heroine becomes so obsessed with her new red shoes that she neglects her duties and can think of nothing else, even in church when she is taking communion. She begins to dance but quickly realizes that she has lost control of her feet. They do what the shoes want to do but, worse, she finds that she cannot stop them dancing. She is saved from being danced to death only by having her feet cut off. The moral of the tale is clear. To fall in love with your appearance is as dangerous as thinking impious thoughts. Both must be chastised for the sake of an ordered society.

Pious and industrious members of society are rewarded, as the Brothers Grimm's 'The Elves and the Shoemaker' shows us. The poor but honest shoe-maker is down to his last piece of leather and, before going to bed, prays for help. The next morning he finds a magnificent pair of shoes in his workroom. They are of such good quality that he sells them for a great deal of money and can buy the leather to resume his trade. This he cuts out and leaves overnight, only to find next day that it has been made into another pair of superb shoes. The process continues for many nights, and eventually the shoemaker and his wife decide to stay up to see how the shoes are made. They hide and, at midnight, two elves appear and stitch the shoes. The shoemaker's wife feels that they must be rewarded and makes two little sets of clothes for them. That night, the elves come and are so thrilled with their new clothes that they dance away and are never seen again.

The concept of help provided by the hands of the little folk is common in many folk tales, but it continues only if humans do not attempt to interfere in any way. What the shoemaker and his wife were guilty of was curiosity. They wished to probe into secret things. Even worse, having probed, they tried to influence matters in the secret world. The obvious connotations are with religious belief in which to acknowledge God without understanding his mysteries is the true act of faith. For our purposes, there is an extra interest in the tale of the cobbler and the elves. He stands for the pious and industrious ideal of a peasant worker, but also serves as a warning to those who wish to meddle in affairs that are not their concern. It is a particularly apt choice of profession – shoemakers were known as thinkers and their history is one of intelligent opposition to social injustice.

Quite apart from references to shoemakers in literature, there are many examples of shoes in their social context. In Jane Austen's *Northanger Abbey* Cathar-ine Morland is being shown around the abbey and notes that 'wherever they went some pattened girl stopped to curtsey', which suggests that pattens were worn by the servant class as a form of tough footwear even if the weather was not inclement. There is a hint of irritation on the part of the well-bred Miss Morland – perhaps the noise upset her delicate sensibilities. In 'The Cricket on the Hearth', Charles Dickens refers to Mrs Perrybingle 'clicking over the wet stones in a pair of pattens that worked innumerable rough impressions of the first proposition in Euclid all about the yard'.

Poets have found the romantic foot in a tiny shoe quite irresistible. Herrick talked of his love's pretty feet which 'like smiles did creep' from under her skirts, while Suckling wrote of his mistress, 'Her feet beneath her petticoat like little mice stole in and out, as if they feared the light.'

Where poets see romance, novelists grasp the opportunity for satire. Jonathan Swift in *Gulliver's Travels* used shoes to symbolize the triviality of party politics. At the court of Lilliput, which stands for Robert Walpole's administration, the two sides are bitterly divided over the question of high versus low heels, 'His majesty hath determined to make use of only low heels in the administration . . . we apprehend his Imperial Highness, the heir to the crown, to have some tendency towards high heels; at least we can plainly discover one of his heels higher than the other, which gives him a hobble in his gait. . . .' Anyone interested in fashion or politics will surely read Swift's words with a strong feeling of recognition.

The link between sex, the foot and the shoe goes back to ancient China. Exactly when the Chinese began to bind the feet of young girls is not recorded but it is popularly linked with the legend of the thirteenth-century Empress Taki who was reputedly born with a club foot. There is a well-established tradition that court circles try as far as possible to ape the mannerisms and even the physical characteristics of royalty so, if the story of the club-footed queen is true, it would explain why it became fashionable at the Chinese court to attempt to minimize the size of the female foot. Fashion is to do with sexual allure and it is axiomatic that the tiny foot remained central to Chinese culture because it was at the centre of the nation's sexuality.

*Fashionable Contrasts; – or – The Duchess's little Shoe yielding to the Magnitude of the Duke's Foot.* Cartoon by James Gillray, 1792

The small foot was achieved by binding the foot at a very early age in order to inhibit growth. This bound foot was known as the Lotus foot and Chinese men have traditionally derived a great deal of their sexual pleasure from it. For them it was in many ways the most important erogenous zone of the female body. Although footbinding of this type is not unknown in other cultures, such a close link between sexuality and the small foot is found only in China.

However, a tightly constrained foot has a place in Western sexuality. Boots which compress the foot and shackle the ankle are frequently seen as having aphrodisiac properties. They go with high heels, which have been synonymous with femininity for a long time. George Bernard Shaw acknowledged as much when he warned women: 'If you rebel against high-heeled shoes, take care to do so in a very smart hat.' The eighteenth-century French literary figure Retif de la Bretonne suggested much the same thing when he said that high heels were part of the true charm of a woman. Even in his day, high-heeled shoes were associated with sex. Many were jewelled up the back and were known as 'venez-y-vair', or 'come-hither', shoes.

The erotic quality of high-heeled shoes goes deeper than mere appearance. Many women say that they feel more sensual in high heels because of the way in which they push the body forward. Certainly, high heels make a woman's walk undulating, which, for many men, is sexually stimulating.

*Femmes fatales* and sex-goddesses rely heavily on high-heeled shoes. It is impossible to imagine Mae West or Marlene Dietrich in sensible shoes of the kind worn by Garbo. Jayne Mansfield and Marilyn Monroe were never seen in the flat pumps worn by Audrey Hepburn. No one would suggest that Garbo and Hepburn lacked sex appeal, but their sexuality was not so overwhelmingly obvious as to account for a high proportion of their screen personality. Sex goddesses deliberately dressed in a way that would make their sexual provocativeness the lasting memory of their fans. Feathers, satin, laced corsets and, inevitably, high-heeled shoes were the ingredients that ensured that the message came over clearly and memorably.

The same ingredients are the stock-in-trade of men who dress as women. Transvestites and drag artists love glamour footwear in shiny black leather or strongly patterned reptile skins. They also favour heels so high that they are almost impossible to walk in. Skin-tight boots reaching to mid-thigh and fastened with laces or studs are particularly popular. Such footwear, which is in fact a grotesque parody of female dress, is also commonly worn by prostitutes.

'Staggerers', as exceptionally high heels are known, are especially erotic for foot fetishists. The shoe as fetish object is not new. Havelock Ellis pointed out that 'of all the forms of erotic symbolism, the most frequent is that which idealizes the foot and shoe', and it is quite clear why. The shoe, especially the high-heeled shoe, combines male and female sexuality in a way which many men and women find irresistible. Perugia, one of this century's greatest shoemakers, said that 'almost every woman is not only conscious of her feet, but sex-conscious about them', and he felt that the creative shoemaker's duty was to add to the foot's sensual powers by imaginative shoe design. Rita de Acosta Lydig, the millionairess style-setter who, in the early years of this century, had her shoes exclusively made for her and kept them as if they were works of art, described a shoe without sex appeal as being as barren as a tree without leaves. Many women would doubtless agree with her but would not assume that sex appeal in shoes depends on high heels. Most men would instantly make that assumption.

Not all fetishists require the objects of their adulation to be overtly sensual in design. Frequently they become excited by shoes simply because they have been worn by the person they love, which is why Goethe wrote to Christine Vulpius, begging her to 'please send me your last pair of shoes, worn out with dancing, as you mentioned in your letter, so that I might have something to press against my heart'.

*The Red Model* by René Magritte, 1935

# SHOES AND SURREALISM

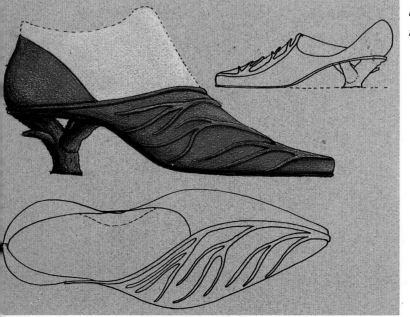

*Above:* Schiaparelli's Shoe Hat, illustrated by Marcel Vertès, 1937

*Below:* Drawings by Regina Martino for the Tree Shoe, 1988

Surrealism is the art movement with a sense of humour so it is not surprising that the Surrealist artists of the 1920s and 1930s responded very quickly to the absurdities of fashion and used them to make witty statements about modern attitudes.

One of the main features of the Surrealist approach is the shock of surprise caused by unexpected juxtapositioning of objects. Schiaparelli's shoe worn on the head as a hat is a classic example of Surrealist wit. Even more perfectly Surrealist is Pierre Cardin's pair of shoes which look like feet and yet are meant to be worn on the feet – the ideal Surrealist double-take.

Other shoemakers have been influenced by the Surrealists' determination to make us look twice and think again about what we see. Regina Martino's Tree Shoe actively plays on associations with shoe-trees as well as visual puns linking leather with bark and wooden heels with tree trunks. Even more amusing are Manolo Blahnik's fantasies based on gloves and Siamese twins. The John Moore advertisement plays on the correspondences between arms and legs, correspondences which the conscious mind prefers to suppress.

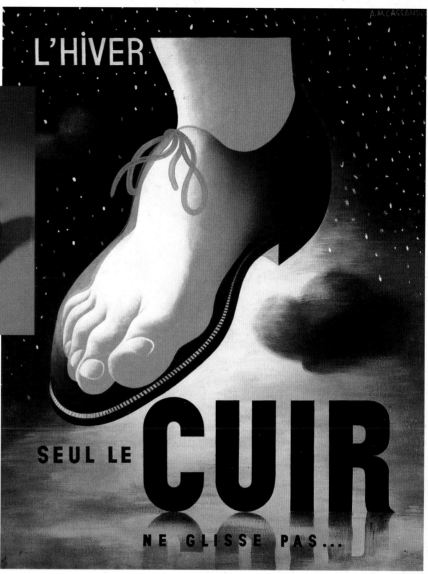

Poster by A. M. Cassandre, 1934

*Above:* Pierre Cardin, Men's Shoes, 1986

Advertisement for John Moore shoes, 1987

Manolo Blahnik, Sketch for the Siamese Twin Shoe, 1989

Manolo Blahnik, Sketch for the Glove Shoes, 1982

# SHOES IN ART

*Original Sin* by Salvador Dali, 1941

*Van Gogh's* Old Boots, *painted in 1886, marks the first attempt by a major painter to portray footwear as a subject worthy of close scrutiny. Painters in previous centuries had often painted shoes and boots with great attention to detail but they were always seen as accessories to the sitter's personality, not as things with a personality of their own. What Van Gogh did was to give inanimate objects a poignancy that pre-shadows Charlie Chaplin's footwear in his early Hollywood films.*

Original Sin, *painted by Salvador Dali in 1941, presents us with a much more complicated message. The boots (old and worn but well-cared for) have been removed in haste – the laces are still tied – and the snake-embellished female foot is obviously the reason. Dali is contrasting the exotic and the humdrum, taking the boots and the naked foot as paradigms of the everyday working life of the male, tied to the earth, and the female, free and unencumbered, ready to take off into worlds exotic and romantic.*

*Right: Old Boots* by Vincent Van Gogh, 1886

# SHOES ON CANVAS

*Lisa Milroy paints portraits of mundane objects in a way that gives them a personality of their own. Here, in one of her many paintings of shoes, close attention reveals variations in what, at first glance, appear to be exact copies of mute objects. The rows of black patent leather pumps are suggestive of separate lives and the shoes have both poignancy and mystery. Are they old or new? From the 1960s or the 1980s? We do not even know if they are pictures of the same pair of shoes or if each image is of a different pair.*

*Allen Jones is also fascinated by the message of shoes but, in his portraits, they are portrayed unequivocally. Their strong personality has a visual impact that almost overwhelms the wearer. The paradox of both painters and their approach to shoes is that, although taking anonymous and undecorated shapes, they imbue them with such a strong character that they remain in the memory.*

*Shoes* by Lisa Milroy, 1986

*Left: First Step* by Allen Jones, 1966

# LACING FOR LUST

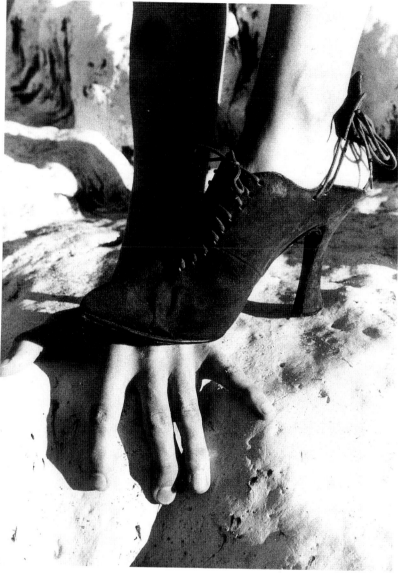

Tight lacing excites desire not just because it has a constraining effect but also because it carries the promise of release. This is why stays have always been such a powerful aphrodisiac. Both the tying and untying can have a strong sexual charge – a fact that shoemakers have been aware of for a very long time. The high-laced boots of the Victorian grande cocotte were unequivocally sexual, as are the modern examples pictured here.

The long, tight boot laced at the side, front or back was so popular in the 1970s that it became a platitude of female fashion. A decade earlier London's Mary Quant had set out to shock with criss-cross corset-laced boots for the sexually liberated woman. She could not have imagined that, a few years later, such a boldly avant-garde attempt to set a trend would end up a cliché.

When tight lacing is applied to men's footwear it still has the frisson of sexual daring which has been lost in women's fashion. The Belgian designer Dirk Bikkembergs has capitalized on homo-erotic fantasies about bondage and domination in order to develop unfamiliar and powerful approaches to male footwear. These boots are the obverse of the male power equation exemplified by Doc Martens. Whereas DMs kit out the male for mastery, the boots on this page suggest a more passive role.

The allure of the shoe which covers the foot but exposes one small area (mules and peep-toed slippers are good examples) is embodied in this creation by Trevor Hill, in which the strong, high-cut front gives no hint of the vulnerability of the open heel.

*Top:* Mary Quant laced boot, late 1960s

*Above:* Shoe by Trevor Hill, 1988

*Opposite:* Boots by Dirk Bikkembergs, Winter 1988-89

# WOMAN INTO SHOE

The fashion artist Antonio Lopez (1943-88) can be credited with almost single-handedly reviving the art of fashion illustration in the early 1980s. His style spawned a multitude of imitators but they all missed his essence. Antonio's work was exceptional because he was not content merely to chronicle the clothes; his drawings captured the fantasy and personality of the creations of the world's great couturiers. He had learned to understand the roots of fashion from Charles James, one of this century's great creative geniuses, when they worked together recording the couturier's life's work.

*Above:* 'Shoe Metamorphosis'
Nancy Lucas, by Antonio, 1978

*Right:* 'Shoe Metamorphosis'
Theresa Spelta, by Antonio, 1978

Antonio's fashion drawings show how, from a firm basis of technical knowledge, he enjoyed pushing visual puns to their limit – never more successfully than in a series of drawings in which he transformed female torsos into shoes while keeping intact the personality of each figure. By simplifying shapes and exaggerating the sweep of curves, Antonio makes the movement from body to shoe seem as natural as it appears inevitable.

'Shoe Metamorphosis' Delia Dougherty, by Antonio, 1978

# SHOES AND SEX

Marlene Dietrich in *The Blue Angel*, 1930

Helmut Berger in *The Damned*, 1969

*Kenneth Tynan described Marlene Dietrich in Joseph von Sternberg's film* The Blue Angel *as singing sardonically of the miseries of licentiousness. The film was made in 1930, and when Visconti made* The Damned *in 1969, he used Helmut Berger in drag to play a parody of the Dietrich part, so adding another layer of decadence.*

*The 1930s drawing by Paul Kamm has the same underlying feeling of excitement, misery and pain. In sex of this kind, whether reality or fantasy, dress is of paramount importance. In all three images the shoes play a crucial role, but it is the boots in the Kamm drawing that most clearly put across the message that danger can often be part of sexual allure.*

Drawing by 'Soulier' (Paul Kamm), c. 1930

# FOOT FETISHISM

*Foot fetishism is not new; it has been a powerful sub-division of sex since shoes were first created. Allen Jones gives his* maîtresse *spiky high heels because he knows that men who associate sexual pleasure with punishment see such heels as symbols of cruelty and pain.*

*Robert Mapplethorpe, whose photographs explored the byways of sex during the 1970s and 1980s, has taken the shoe fetishist's desire to kiss and lick his partner's shoes to its final conclusion.*

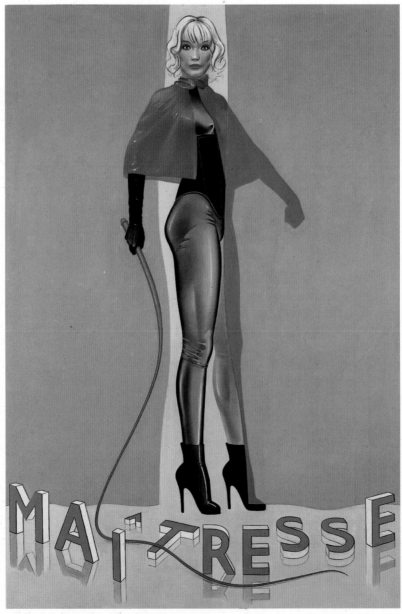

Poster by Allen Jones for the film *Maîtresse*, 1976

*Opposite: Ken Moody with Shoe* by Robert Mapplethorpe, 1985

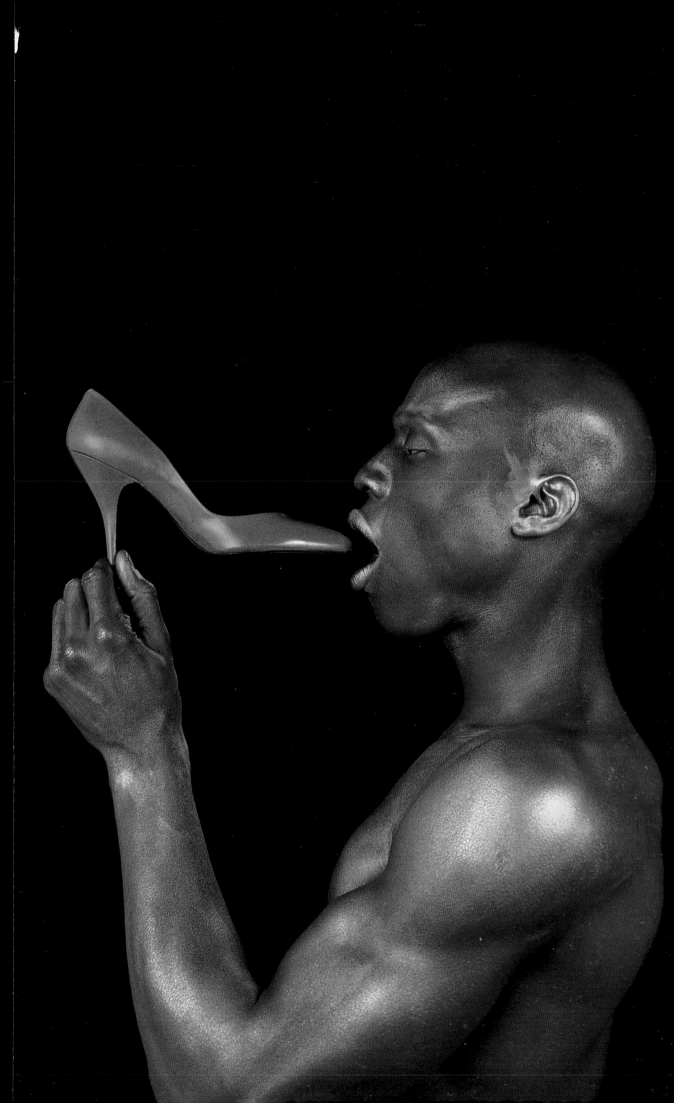

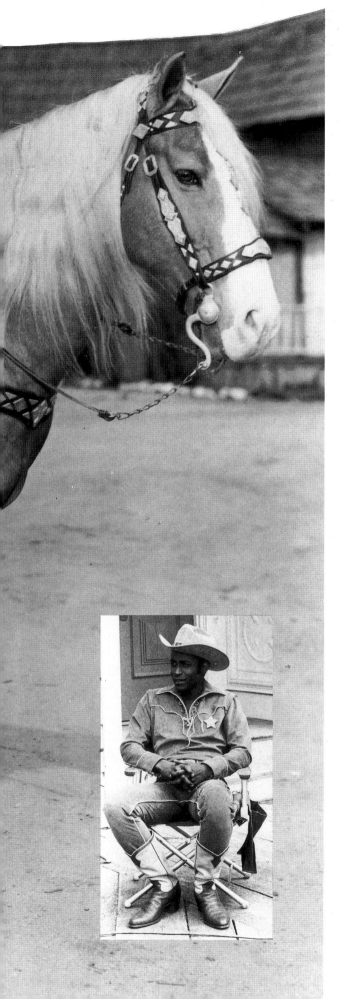

# COWBOY BOOTS

*Cowboys were a showbusiness invention. The tough, hardworking cowhands who were employed in the early years of the nineteenth century to drive cattle across the plains to the slaughterhouses of cities like Chicago were anything but romantic heroes and had little in common with the icons of masculinity in the Hollywood films of the 1920s and 1930s. The celluloid creations were glamorous; the reality was not. Gene Autry and Roy Rogers were dressed like fashion plates to ride the range – no sweat or dust was allowed to sully their immaculately pure image.*

*Luckily, Hollywood has always been saved from total banality by its ability to laugh at the absurdity of its own creations and the western got what was coming to it in* Blazing Saddles, *with its 'designer' sheriff who not only had a black skin – he also had a customized Gucci saddle.*

*Even so, for sheer decorative inventiveness, the saddle in that film could not compare with the cowboy boots of the stars of the thirties and forties. The boots worn here by Roy Rogers represent many hours of skilled work by master craftsmen and prove that US cowboy bootmakers of the thirties were following the true traditions of folk art, as their Texas counterparts are still doing today . . .*

*Top left:* Second Guard. Cowboys at night awakening their relief watch

*Main picture:* Roy Rogers

*Left:* Pause during filming of *Blazing Saddles*, 1974

# URBAN COWBOY

Plain black buckle boot by Western Styling, 1989

Traditional brown lizard-skin boot by Paul Smith, 1989

# EASY RIDERS

As the falsity of the traditional film cowboy as male hero was exposed, the new-style, urban cowboy took his place in the iconography of heroism. Instead of a horse he rode a motorbike, which was customized every bit as elaborately as Roy Rogers' saddle and boots.

   The boots of the easy riders were, like their wearers, a paler version of the cowboy's, stripped of most of the decoration. They were not quite as brutal as the version worn by the urban despatch riders of the eighties, which give them the appearance (and walk) of beings from another planet.

*Right:* Dennis Hopper and Peter Fonda in *Easy Rider*, 1969

*Below:* Marlon Brando in *The Wild One*, 1954

*Inset:* Motorcycle messengers, London, 1989

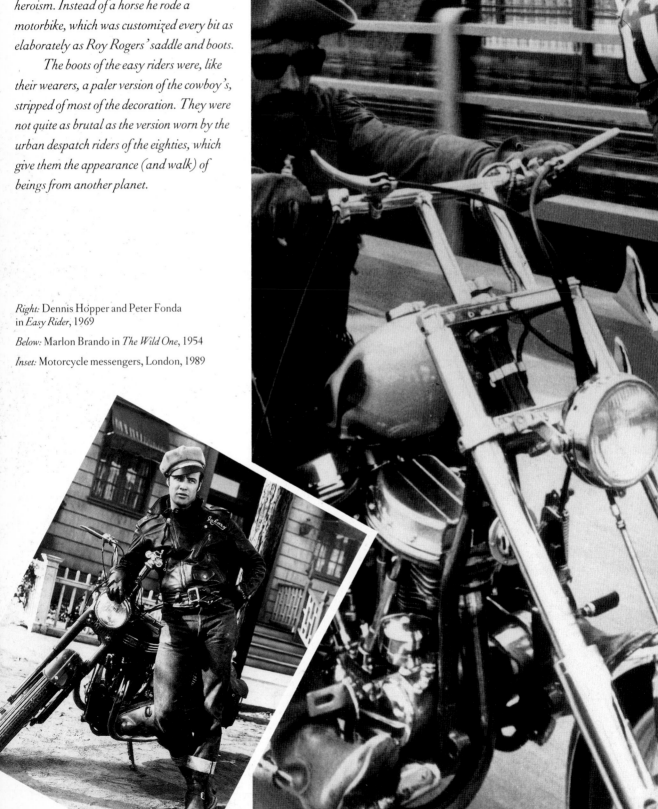

# SHOES AND MAGIC

The Old Woman Who Lived in a Shoe, from *Old Nursery Rhymes*, illustrated by Lawson Wood, 1933

*The magical qualities attributed to shoes have given them a central role in many fairytales. Just as human beings have been preoccupied with dreams of escape by flight, so they have woven fantasies in which shoes and boots have been the instruments of escape from humdrum and victimized lives.*

*Seven League Boots, Puss in Boots: the magical power that gives the ordinary and humble the ability to move out of their environment into a better world is the traditional reward for donning these talismanic items. In fact, the magical power of boots is the age-old equivalent to the modern story-teller's obsession with the spacecraft that can take ordinary boys and girls beyond the bounds of human possibilities and safely into another world.*

*Various models have been suggested for the heroine of the children's rhyme The Old Woman Who Lived in a Shoe, including Caroline, wife of George II, who had eight children, and Elizabeth Vergoose of Boston who had ten stepchildren and six of her own. Iona and Peter Opie, in their* Encyclopaedia of Nursery Rhymes, *remark the consistency between the custom of casting a shoe after a bride in the wish that the union should be fruitful and the extraordinary fertility of the old woman who actually inhabited a shoe.*

Seven League Boots, from Perrault's *Fairy Tales*, illustrated by Gustave Doré, 1862

Puss in Boots, from Perrault's *Fairy Tales*, illustrated by Gustave Doré, 1863

# *THE GLASS SLIPPER*

*Cinderella is the most popular of all fairy tales. Hundreds of versions exist, but the 1697 rendering by Charles Perrault is the first in which the glass slipper makes an appearance. A slipper made of glass seemed an odd idea to Perrault's later editors; they changed it to fur, assuming* verre *(glass) to be a misprint for* vair *(miniver). Perhaps it was. If so, it was an inspired error since a glass shoe – fragile and unstretchable – seems the most rigorous test of perfect fit. Its transparency and preciousness also make it the ideal symbol both of Cinderella's purity and of the luxury that her small foot was to win her.*

*Opposite:* Illustration from Perrault's *Tales of Passed Times by Mother Goose*, 1796

*Above:* Illustration by Harry Clarke from Perrault's *Fairy Tales*, 1922

*Right:* From Walt Disney's *Cinderella*, 1950

*Far right: Cinderella*, performed by the Princesses Elizabeth and Margaret, Windsor Castle, 21 December 1941

# LUCKY SHOES

*There are few countries that do not have some superstition involved with footwear as a good luck talisman in the area of love and marriage. The most common is the tradition – based on the shoe as a symbol of fertility – of tying an old boot to the back of the vehicle taking newly weds to their new home or off on their honeymoon. A shoe was chosen because it represented not only fruitfulness, but also stability, prosperity and harmony. The implication was that shoes betokened comfort and warmth – both considered desirable for a happy marriage.*

*The same idea was behind the custom, especially popular in the nineteenth century, of giving china and pottery miniatures of shoes and boots as good luck charms to friends and relations, often to mark important family occasions such as christenings, anniversaries and birthdays. In both cases the shoe was taken to represent and, at the same time, encourage the domestic virtues. It is not by accident that Judy Garland as Dorothy in* The Wizard of Oz *wears her ruby shoes for good luck and is told by Glenda, the Good Witch, 'Close your eyes and tap you heels together three times and think to yourself, "there's no place like home".' The instructions are precisely in the mainstream of superstitious thinking about shoes.*

*However, magic shoes are not always benign. In the film* The Red Shoes, *made in 1948 and starring Moira Shearer, the heroine's elegant scarlet ballet shoes were so malevolent that they literally danced her to death.*

*Above:* Jack Haley, Ray Bolger, Judy Garland and Bert Lahr in *The Wizard of Oz*, 1939

Maid tying boot to the back of a wedding vehicle, 1940s

Blue and white boot in faience, Bayreuth, 1745-47

Good Luck shoe, Delft, Holland, early 18th century

*Opposite page:* Moira Shearer in *The Red Shoes*, 1948

# THE ROYAL WALK

The royal walk is one of total confidence. It proceeds from the absolute assurance that there will be no let or hindrance to the stately progress. On one of the rare occasions when there was, Sir Walter Raleigh was on hand with his cloak to overcome the problem. Since that day, royalty has surged forward with scarcely a glance down.

　　The shoes of royalty need to combine glamour and comfort. In this century three generations of British queens have put their trust in H & M Rayne, their 'by appointment' shoemakers who understand the need to balance theatricality with regality.

　　Royal heels must be sufficiently high to ensure that even the smallest stands out; there is no point in royalty being present if they cannot be seen. The Princess of Wales is the first member of the British royal family for many years for whom this has not posed a problem.

*Left:* Lady Crosfield and the Duchess of York (now the Queen Mother) attending a tennis tournament, 1925

*Top Centre:* Princess Elizabeth and the Duke of Edinburgh inspecting the guard of honour formed by the Junior Training Corps of Elizabeth College, Guernsey, 1949

*Top right:* Elizabeth, wife of George VI, approaching St Paul's Cathedral to attend a service, 1949

*Right:* The Princess of Wales attending Royal Ascot, 1988

# MULES

The mule – a high-heeled, backless slipper – has fallen from grace over the centuries. Originally it evolved as a form of footwear for the boudoir, worn by the most fashionable of ladies and the most exclusive of courtesans, but the twentieth century has seen it debased to such an extent that its sexual message is almost totally seedy, downtown and cheap. In fact, television and film producers seem automatically to use mules as a form of shorthand. Worn by an actress of any age the message is clear: virtue lost, or about to be, without any regrets.

Interestingly enough, Manet's Olympia, completely naked apart from a bracelet, a neck cord and satin mules, looks much less salacious than Marilyn Monroe with her slinky, feather-trimmed dress, phallic cigarette and furry peep-toed mules. The inference to be drawn from her footwear is very obvious.

Whatever glamour mules may still retain hardly survives mass-production for the cheap market. Such products, with tacky fur or feather trim, often in day-glo colours, seem to have lost for ever any of the romantic connotations they had in past centuries.

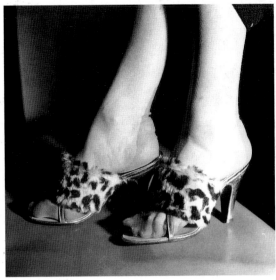

*Above:* Mules created for Spring, 1954
*Right:* Elvis Presley and Judy Tyler in *Jailhouse Rock*, 1957

*Below: Olympia* by Edouard Manet, 1863
*Far right:* Marilyn Monroe in *The Seven Year Itch*, 1955

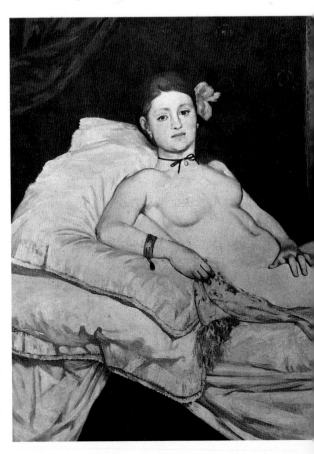

SPAIN PROVIDES A proof that man adopted footwear at a very early stage of his development. Cave paintings found there, dated between 12,000 and 15,000 BC, show a man in boots of skin and a woman in boots of fur. Persian funerary jars of around 3000 BC made in the shapes of boots show that the basic forms of ancient footwear – the foot wrapping of skin and the primitive sandal – were already in existence by this time.

In Egypt, sandals from the 1st century AD, made of woven palm leaves bound at the edges, were little more than a flat sole with thongs at the ankle and toes. Egyptian sandals from a later period have soles carved from a solid block of wood, much like the European pattens of the seventeenth century. It is not known if these sandals were in general wear; they may have been used only to give the feet extra protection when the Nile flooded. In the Bally Museum at Schoenenwerd, in Switzerland, there is a sixth-century wooden-soled Etruscan sandal which is split and hinged with leather for greater flexibility and comfort. This shows a degree of sophistication which many European patten makers did not possess. Seventeenth-century hinged examples of pattens are comparatively rare.

*The Swing* by Jean-Honoré Fragonard, c. 1766

Late Palaeolithic wall paintings from caves in Eastern Spain

Palm leaf sandal from Thebes, before 1250 BC

The Etruscans were probably the most advanced shoemakers until the Greeks and Romans. They took the primitive idea of creating a covering for the foot by wrapping a skin around it and refined it to produce a prototype of the early brogue. This was sole-less, split at the instep and tied with a lace. It remained a standard shoe for peasants up to the time of Charlemagne.

It is important to remember that early shoe styles continued unaltered for centuries, but by the fourth century there was a cross-fertilization which produced decorative variations from different parts of the Mediterranean world. Traders from Greece, Spain and Cyprus who had visited Egypt and Syria would return with details of the customs and costumes they had seen, and their own dress would have been noted in the ports they called on.

Centuries later, as the Dark Ages receded, the same kind of cross-over of ideas occurred in Europe, brought about mainly by merchants and traders who travelled the Continent and beyond in their search for markets and supplies. However, by this time there was an additional source of information through the courtiers and diplomats who moved between the newly emerged countries and city states to arrange protective treaties, trade agreements and advantageous marriages.

The courts of the Middle Ages were stylish and fashion-conscious. On returning from their missions, emissaries and plenipotentiaries were eagerly questioned about the fashions at rival courts. By the fourteenth century the court fashion for wearing soled hose competed with, but did not supersede, the use of shoes, which were sufficiently prized for their workmanship to be protected by galoshes during the winter. The fourteenth-century courtly ideal of beauty and grace produced *The Romance of the Rose* and the belief in the importance of chivalry. Beauty of appearance was an essential component of the new thinking which was more refined, in all senses, than anything since the days of ancient Greece.

The ambition of princes was manifested in the magnificence of their attire and it produced impressively jewelled ceremonial footwear, although the most powerful shoe fashion remained the poulaine. By the beginning of the sixteenth century, costly and sumptuous dress was increasingly apparent at court and the duck's-bill shoe which had replaced the poulaine was modified into the heelless eschapin, the front of which was frequently slashed, often showing a coloured lining underneath.

As the century advanced, courtly dress became increasingly vulgar. Ostentatious and over-decorative, it perfectly reflected the newfound confidence of kings. Although far from easy in their beds, they were less likely to be violently deposed than at any time in the previous two hundred years. By the beginning of the seventeenth century, elaborate masques and dances had become a feature of court life. Their object was to glorify the king and make his position appear unassailable. That Charles I and Louis XVI both ended on the block shows that the move was not entirely successful.

The royal families in the sixteenth and seventeenth centuries were the true arbiters of taste. What they approved was worn; what they refused to sanction was not. They were also leaders of fashion. When Henri II of Lorraine wore his magnificent cuffed boots and boot hose trimmed with lace, he was setting a style which those of his courtiers who could afford to would immediately emulate. The soft leather boots favoured by Henri IV became so elegant that they were actually accepted in salons by the beginning of the seventeenth century. When Louis XIV wore red heels, everybody who frequented the court copied them. Some courtly fashions defied imitation: Empress Elizabeth Petrovna, the daughter of Peter the Great, was attended by Arab boys in ankle-high boots with upturned toes and extravagant ribbon bows. Such an ostentatious style could endanger the position of a courtier who tried to copy it.

Other fashions cried out to be imitated. Louis XV's mistress, Madame de Pompadour, had tiny feet. To accentuate them she wore high heels that curved into a small base. Inevitably known as Pompadour heels, they were adopted by the ladies of the court who even went so far as to bind their feet with tape so that their daintiness might be noticed by the King. Marie Antoinette's fashion mania is well-known. No court lady could possibly emulate her. She had shoes for every outfit and had them catalogued so that her servants could keep control of them.

Marie Antoinette's extravagance was extreme even perhaps for royalty but her obsession with her appearance was not unique. Napoleon knew how to dress for success, and so have many recent members of royal families. In this century, the most successful royal trendsetter must surely be Edward, Prince of Wales.

Man's tan Russian calf and white buckskin spectator (co-respondent) shoe, c.1935

The Prince of Wales popularized spectator shoes – albeit for a rather 'fast' type of man; he surprised America by wearing white shoes on his visit there, but probably his most spectacular breakthrough in shoe fashion was to make suede acceptable for semi-formal town wear. Again, only the young and carefree took to it. Loelia, Duchess of Westminster, recalled in her memoirs that her father considered suede shoes the sign of a cad and a bounder.

When the Prince of Wales renounced the throne and his brother became George VI, his consort Queen Elizabeth seemed very unstylish after the elegant Wallis Simpson. However, the Queen soon evolved a style of her own that was more distinctive and original than anything seen in royal circles before or since. Following Queen Mary's lead, she appointed H & M Rayne as her shoemaker. Taking advantage of a swing towards wedge heels and platform soles in the late 1930s and 1940s, she dramatically increased her height by having Rayne create shoes with six-inch heels and platform soles. Queen Elizabeth especially liked white shoes, preferably in calf or suede. With peep-toes, sling backs and ankle straps, they were intensely feminine. However, they were not always the most practical footwear. On the South African tour taken by the Royal Family in 1946, crossing rough terrain, one of the Queen's shoes broke and Princess Elizabeth, who was wearing flat walking shoes, took them off and gave them to her mother with the remark, 'How typical of Mummy'. It is probably the only time Queen Elizabeth, the Queen Mother, has ever been seen on an official occasion wearing anything but high heels.

For royal tours in the 1950s, wardrobes were extensive and every outfit had its own pair of shoes designed especially to complement the occasion and the dress to be worn for it. Rayne would be informed of the colours and materials of the dresses being designed by Hartnell and Amies and would present sketches of styles for Queen Elizabeth, the Queen Mother, and the Queen to decide which were to be made. Things are much simpler now, and the Queen Mother has rationalized her shoe requirements. She has only two styles – one for evening and one for day. When she orders new shoes, the instructions are brief. Her lady-in-waiting need only tell Rayne that, for example, one evening style is required in pale grey silk, and the firm can produce it.

The Queen has always taken a more practical approach to fashion than her mother and actually calls her wardrobe 'clothes for going about my business'. Her heels are of medium height and the foot is shaped for comfort. Like most of the Queen's clothes, her shoes are basically a modified fifties fashion and, as such, are very similar to the styles bought from the top 'up-market' shoe retail chains in their millions by middle-aged, middle-class women worldwide. The Queen has followed this century's royal pattern of dressing perfectly suitably but not exceptionally.

The concept of a royal fashion leader has revived in the eighties with the Princess of Wales. She has broken from tradition in not having her shoes specially designed for her, and, although she still buys from Rayne, she does not confine herself to one manufacturer. Except for very special occasions, she chooses from ready-to-wear ranges, sometimes requesting a particular colour or an exclusive trim. Her preference for low-heeled, simple pumps is well-known and is shared by her 'Sloane Ranger' contemporaries but, for evening wear, the Princess opts for glamour, choosing thin-strapped dancing sandals in silver and gold.

Although royalty as a fashion influence has all but gone, this does not mean that there are no longer arbiters of taste. Quite apart from the enormous influence of the couturiers, it must be remembered that the influence of high society is still a strong one. It is an influence that, during this century, has moved from Europe to the United States. What Jackie Kennedy and Nancy Reagan wore when they were wives of presidents has had an influence comparable with that of crowned heads in the past. Their clothes, including the style of their shoe, were copied far beyond their immediate circle.

*Below, top to bottom:* Oxford, Derby, Brogue, d'Orsay, Pump

Increased democracy and improved living standards have meant that the gap between rich and poor has appreciably narrowed and, for the first time in history, the working classes – the majority of any country's population – are able to experience fashion. Mass fashion exists when enough people have money and leisure to make a choice. That is what makes fashion change possible.

The most interesting development as far as shoes are concerned is that this choice is so wide. Because shoe fashions change slowly and a new shoe style does not automatically spell the demise of previous styles, most shoe shops throughout the Western world carry a range of styles covering many years. It is possible to find walking shoes in shapes barely altered since the 1940s, sandals made on lasts designed in the 1950s and stiletto heels from the 1960s. Only the styles of the 1970s are considered old-fashioned both because they were very strong and extreme and because the decade is too close to ours to have benefitted from the perspective of time. It is an interesting fact that, even now, more women buy the court pump of the 1950s than any other current available style.

Mass-production enables shoe manufacturers to produce new styles at competitive prices, but all these styles are, in fact, variations on themes. In non-specialist terms there are eight basic footwear types from which all men's and women's styles are created. The Oxford is a laced shoe, with its vamp stitched to the quarters, which are joined by the lacing. In the Derby, also known as the Blucher and Gibson, the vamp continues under the quarters to form a tongue over which the laces are tied. The Brogue is similar to the Oxford, but is heavily pinked and perforated where the vamp and quarters meet and has decorative additions. The d'Orsay dips to a V at either side of the shoe. The Pump is the lowest cut of all styles. The feminine version, with a high heel, is known in the U.K. as a Court. The Boot is a style which normally reaches above the ankle, but it includes the Jodhpur, which reaches to the ankle. The Moccasin, originally made of buckskin, is the archetype for all slip-on footwear. It is low-cut at the sides with a raised, stitched vamp. The Sandal is an open shoe held on the foot by straps or thongs.

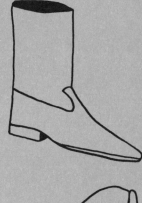

Within these shapes, ingenious designers can create a huge range of styles. In the last forty years there have been more than in all earlier centuries put together. Advanced technical knowledge has enabled designers to achieve previously impossible conceits such as the heelless high-heeled shoe or the entirely transparent 'Cinderella' slipper. A shoe designer can introduce a wide range of design features merely by experimenting with the shape of the shoe, quite apart from additional decorative trims.

There is a seemingly infinite number of ways of treating the heel. It can be aggressive, ingratiating, sculptural or aerodynamic. The most elegant heel is surely the stiletto, now rightly frowned on for the damage it can cause, but still representing a perfectly engineered shape. The front of a shoe, especially the toe, presents the other opportunity for design originality: it can be rounded, pointed, squared-off, slanted, flattened, raised – and decorated with pinking, slashing, draping or mixed colours or materials.

For many designers, the material of a shoe is the greatest stimulus and yet even today, despite the considerable advances in the development of man-made substitutes, the majority of Western shoes have uppers of leather. Traditional leather soles are now usually found only in the higher-priced ranges; cheaper shoes have composite or injection-moulded plastic soles.

The choice of materials mirrors the division between the sexes as sharply as it did in the eighteenth century. Men's shoes are predominantly made with leather uppers – chrome, kid, patent, suede or brushed pigskin – a reflection of men's conservative tastes and desire for practicality. Women's shoes are far more adventurous. The use of brocades, cut velvets, satins, moire silks, wool, crewel work and beaded materials is not new – these have been fabrics for women's shoes since the sixteenth century. What is new is the modern use of skins such as fish, ostrich, crocodile, alligator and even terrapin. Every possible kind of snakeskin has been experimented with, as well as the skins of the 'big cats', with leopard proving a special favourite. During the 1980s there was a revulsion against the use of animal skin and fur in fashion. The public now prefers imitations. Jazzy fake leopard and tiger skins and convincing reptile substitutes retain the glamour without disturbing the conscience.

*Above, top to bottom:* Boot, Moccasin, Sandal

Quite apart from skins and fabrics, the surface of the shoe has frequently been printed or painted. In the thirties Ferragamo painted his shoes and Tokio Kumagai, in the eighties, hand-decorated shoes in the styles of major twentieth-century artists, such as Dali and Mondrian. Hand-decorated shoes cost a fortune, but decorative effects using screen printing bring the fantasy within everyone's range. Shoes printed with newsprint, cartoon characters and *trompe l'oeil* effects regularly reappear when fashion has moved into a jokey or nostalgic phase.

Such extravagant treatments are normally reserved for women's shoes – but it was not always the case. In the past, men have enjoyed highly decorated shoes just as much as women. The seventeenth-century roses which they wore on their shoes grew to enormous proportions and were made in the finest of materials. A man of stature would have his roses trimmed with gold lace, pearls and spangles in order to impress. The shoe buckles which took their place were much more sober and understated, but by the middle of the eighteenth century they were a true status symbol, telling at a glance the wealth, position and taste of the wearer. A man of style might have as many as fifty different types – plain silver or silver gilt for everyday wear and bejewelled with precious stones for special occasions – including cut jet for funerals.

Jewelers and shoemakers found it difficult to keep up with the demands for novelty designs, such as 'Whim Wham', 'Crow's Foot', or 'Job's Fancy.' Buckles became a universal fashion, although the Artois, the most fashionable of all, which was introduced by the Comte d'Artois in the 1750s, being large and made of coiled silver, was well beyond the pocket of all but the wealthy.

Most men were prudent and, instead of walking the streets with buckles twinkling with real diamonds, chose to have them set with paste. Fops went to such extremes that they could only afford paste. Sheridan pointed out that although buckles had originally been a practical fastening, the point had been reached where 'the shoe is of no earthly use but to keep on the buckle'.

In England, the industry producing buckles was largely centered around Birmingham and is estimated to have employed as many as 40,000 people, so it was a great economic blow when the 'effeminate shoestring' superseded them. Attempts to stop the fashion had no effect, even though the Prince of Wales was petitioned not to wear laces and, for a time, continued with buckles. They were preserved for court dress and were still worn by men on official court occasions up to the 1950s. However, even without the advent of laces, the life of buckles was doomed because by the beginning of the 1800s boots were increasingly taking over from shoes as the fashionable wear for men.

It must be remembered, of course, that boots had always been the style for workers. Working boots were crude and tough and it was not until this century that they began to assume an aura of glamour. The first workboot to be romanticized was the cowboy boot. The modern concept of the cowboy as the working gentleman and hero, honest and true, is of course a myth perpetuated by Hollywood, but it is so convincing that men have often adopted cowboy dress even when they did not know one end of a horse from the other. Suede fringed jackets, blue jeans and roughly woven check shirts reached a peak of fashionability after World War II, but quite the most sought-after items of cowboy costume were the boots. The western wear phenomenon cannot be lightly dismissed. It is America's great contribution to twentieth-century dress, first introduced to Parisian halls of fashion by Jacques Fath in 1949, after a visit to Texas, and endlessly recycled.

Early cowboy boots had no ornamentation. They evolved from the riding boots of the Mexican *vaquero*, but, for control in the saddle, the shoe portion was made so tight that walking was difficult and painful. As both boots were made on the same last, they needed breaking in, and there are stories of cowboys standing in troughs of water to soften the leather so that it would take the shape of the foot. The cowboy boot of inlaid leather with decorative stitching did not become the fashionable archetype until Tom Mix made it popular in his films of the 1920s.

The power of the screen cowboy's image influenced the boots of real cow-hands who performed at rodeos. Stitching, toe styles, colours and inlaid work were copied from film design – and then copied again for 'fancy' boots worn by men on the streets. An industry grew up. Designs became increasingly showy, using alligator, waxed calf, lizard, python and even kangaroo skins. By the 1950s, the common decorative devices, which required a high level of handcraftsmanship, included abstract Indian patterns, Long Horns, cacti, panoramic desert pictures and maps of the Lone Star State.

The highest level of the bootmaker's art, in the opinion of many, had been reached in the 1940s by the Lucchese Company of Texas, which produced forty-eight pairs of boots to symbolize each of the states, featuring inlays of the state house and the state flower, bird and flag. Not that fancy 'one-offs' were new in the cowboy boot business: Charlie Dunn, one of Texas's most famous makers, had produced in 1914 a pair of boots trimmed with gold and inlaid with diamonds and rubies for a gambler who paid him $5,000. Many U.S. presidents have felt it expedient to have a pair of cowboy boots made. In 1948, Harry Truman ordered his from Tony Lama, who called the design 'El Presidente'. This fashion was followed by Dwight Eisenhower, Lyndon Johnson, Jimmy Carter and Ronald Reagan.

The cowboy boot is not alone as a working style removed from its environment and taught to speak a new language. The high-laced American combat boot has also transferred to the streets, along with camouflaged jackets and marines' khaki trousers. Semiotically, it shares the same roots as the Doc Marten, which has been aptly described as a boxing glove for the foot. Both have achieved a considerable following among urban young men excited by the violence of battles they have not experienced. These are aggressive boots which have not been cosmeticized and neutralized as the cowboy boot has. They were not initially designed for aggression. Dr Klaus Maertens, of Munich, created his famous air-cushioned soles in 1945 because, having broken his foot while skiing, he needed a comfortable sole. He started to produce the sole commercially in 1947 but it was not until 1960 that the Dr Maertens shoes, designed for comfort, evolved into Doc Martens, destined to be used for violence.

Urban warriors are a phenomenon of the eighties and they are the product of the decade's increasing violence. Societies are fragmented as a result not only of actual wars, but also of ideological battles. In the West in this century, there have been few open revolutions, but there have been many quiet revolutions. These bloodless battles have to do with the position of youth vis-à-vis age and women in relation to men. They still continue.

A battle which seems already to have been won is the fight against formality, the results of which are seen most obviously in clothes. Hats, gloves, veils, stiff collars, formal suits and ties – when the century dawned they were *de rigueur* (for all but the poorest) on Sundays, high days and festivals. In the 1930s, Stanley Holloway, the Cockney comedian, had a popular monologue about a working-class man who wore brown boots to a funeral – a shocking sartorial solecism fully understood by his listeners. Nowadays, it would hardly be noticed. In the 1970s informality became entwined with the cult of health, with a marked effect on footwear. Jane Fonda put 'working out' on the map; aerobics and jogging caught the imagination of all age groups and city parks were suddenly full of young and old taking exercise. The result was that special footwear which had been devised for athletes was bought in millions of pairs by people newly 'hooked' on exercise. To keep demand high, the giants like Adidas, Puma and Nike produced what were virtually fashion ranges. Every season saw new design modifications, colour combinations and logos, most of which were sales promotion ruses and had little to do with improving the efficiency of the shoe for exercise.

Inevitably, the exercise craze passed, but the demand for training shoes, known as trainers, did not. Young people liked them for their informality and older people liked them because they were broad-based and cushion-soled and so accommodated the foot in comfort. Everyone liked them because they were cheaper than traditional shoes. Trainers have now become a cliché on our city streets. Although essentially casual wear, they are worn quite unselfconsciously with suits by men and with town clothes by women, even though they look ugly and out of scale with such clothes. Their huge popularity has raised a question mark in the shoe business. It is perfectly conceivable that by the end of the next decade traditional informal styles such as the moccasin, loafer and ankle boot will have been routed by the all-conquering trainer.

Training shoes have an additional attraction because of their link with the growth of the sportsman as popular hero. In the early seventies, young fashion was influenced by pop music but, as television moguls realized that sport commanded even bigger audiences, pop heroes surrendered the limelight to athletic folk heroes. During the eighties the trend intensified. The extravagant footwear of the pop scene has largely gone. The video *Dancing in the Street* features Mick Jagger and David Bowie, two of pop's longest lasting stars, wearing sneakers of the kind that manufacturers have now dubbed athletic footwear. The 'ath-leisure' fashion, as it is sometimes known, is aimed squarely at the young, so it is linked with both music and sport in order to capitalize on the twin cultural forces of the market. Athletic footwear is normally white and, high-top or low-top, it increasingly resembles baseball boots.

Makers have been quick to realize that exposure and endorsement boost sales. They have noticed that sharp young cinema-goers are aware that Eddie Murphy wore Adidas in *Beverly Hills Cop* and that the dancers in *A Chorus Line* were in Puma. Increasingly, manufacturers pay middle-men considerable sums to guarantee product placement in top-audience youth films. At the same time, sports stars like Chris Evert and baseball super-hero Michael Jordan are signed up to promote new lines. The market aimed at is the most volatile in the world: inner-city youth, mainly black, Hispanic or Asian, who now account for more than 20 percent of sales in the ath-leisure field.

The turnover is quick: shelf life of a new product can be as little as three weeks and rarely lasts for more than two and a half months. Anything that the youth market deems not 'fresh' dies. The market has been dominated by rap dancing and the famous rap group Run D.M.C. had a hit in 1987 with a song called 'My Adidas' – proof indeed of the cult status of athletic footwear.

Cleaning shoes, 30 June 1945

# FERRAGAMO'S MATERIALS

Salvatore Ferragamo was a shoemaker of great ingenuity – his delight in breaking the rules is nowhere more apparent than in his work with new materials. Only a master could so confidently exploit many materials that had never before been used in shoemaking. During World War II, for example, when leather was in short supply, Ferragamo substituted cellophane for the body of the shoe. For soles, he triumphantly revived the use of cork and wood. The selection of materials on these pages shows Ferragamo's range in the 1930s, 1940s, and 1950s.

*Above left:* Beige 'pilor' with brown grosgrain

*Above:* Yellow, red and pale green silk threads

*Far left:* Gilded glass mosaic sole and satin and calf strap

*Left:* Natural hemp and plaited cords of polychrome

*Right:* Elasticized white silk with gold brocade effect

*Below:* Woven polychrome raffia

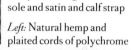

*Top:* Sea-leopard in orange, green, blue and yellow

*Centre:* Ostrich skin divided by calf strip

*Bottom:* Synthetic raffia worked in crochet

*Above:* Cords of plaited bark

*Left:* Carved and painted wood

*Right:* Multi-coloured crocheted cellophane

*Right:* Black antelope with plaited circular decoration bordered with chain stitch in silk

*Below:* Canvas embroidered in geometric design with polychrome cotton thread

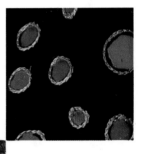

*Above:* Woven grass from the Philippines

*Right:* Bordeaux crocodile

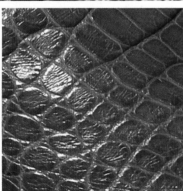

*Above:* Beige tinted fish-skin

*Below:* 18-carat gold

*Top left:* Small rosette buckles from 1920

*Top right:* Engraved portrait of Samuel Bernard, by P. Drevet, after Rigaud, 1729

*Bottom left:* Fashionable women at Longchamps, 1919

*Bottom right:* Portrait of Countess Howe by Thomas Gainsborough (1727-88)

# BUCKLES

Buckled shoes were originally a male conceit. On 22 January 1660, Samuel Pepys proudly noted in his diary, 'This day I began to put on buckles to my shoes' – an event singular enough to warrant entering. Buckles were originally a rich man's pleasure, meant to proclaim his particularity to the more middling and lower classes. They were frequently made of silver and set with precious stones. Never an integral part of a shoe, they were transferred from one pair to another and were generally treated as pieces of jewelry.

Although they were a very obvious part of the male arsenal of personal display, buckles were not solely confined to men; they were equally popular with women in the eighteenth century. Many of the most richly decorated and embroidered shoes for both sexes that have survived from previous centuries were designed to be worn with buckles, though the buckles have rarely survived with them. It should be remembered that despite all of the opportunities for ostentatious display afforded by impressive buckles they were essentially a practical method of fastening a shoe and, as such, they went into a decline when lacing and buttoning became more fashionable.

Although buckles have been revived frequently, especially in this century, they have normally been used as a decorative device fixed to a shoe which is closed and kept on the foot by other methods, though in the twenties and thirties buckles were used as an alternative to buttons on women's shoes and sandals. They still survive in their most mundane form as fastenings for sandals and casual shoes worn by men and children.

*Left:* Portrait of John Plampin by Thomas Gainsborough, 1755

109

# HEIGHTS OF FASHION

The raised shoe has been around for centuries. In the past, lifting the foot above ground level was often a practical measure, providing protection from the mud and dirt of unmetalled roads. The original patten, with its iron ring underneath, was created for this purpose and the hollowed out chopine, slap sole and overshoe performed the same function.

In the twentieth century raised soles serve no utilitarian purpose. In fact, they are now viewed as the most impractical of styles. But shoe designers love them because they give them space to play decorative games. Ferragamo's 1930s interpretations of the Venetian chopine reached new heights of extravagance. Less elegant, but far more ubiquitous, were the platforms of the 1970s.

*Left:* Ferragamo sandal with
platform sole and heel in
cork layers covered in
suede, 1938

*Above left:* Design for a Florentine
Intermezzo by Bernardo Buontalenti,
1589

*Above right:* Silvano Malta/Antonelli,
1971

*Left above:* Girl's shoe with blocks at
toe and heel, Italy, before 1600

*Left below:* Women's shoe with
overshoe, France, before 1715

# DECORATIVE DEVICES

*From earliest times, successful footwear has balanced the decorative and the practical. The Romans gilded and chased their sandals; in the sixteenth century slippers were made of rich velvets and fine silks; eighteenth-century noblemen covered their mules with brocade and embroidery; the Victorians trimmed their boots with jet and lace. Even in periods when function appears to override fantasy, as in the 1820s or the 1920s, the decorative urge cannot be stilled.*

*The designer has the greatest scope for fantasy when making shoes primarily for indoor or evening wear.*

*There are three things to consider: shape, material and decoration. In the examples on these pages we see how they have been tackled at different periods.*

*The Victorian satin slipper and the Roger Vivier shoe have the same elegant curved heel and high instep. The Johnny Moke shoe has a heel gracefully counterbalanced between a straight line and a curve. The decorative trim on each shoe is strongly eye-catching and the materials – satin, brocade and velvet – have a tactile quality that adds an extra dimension to the pleasure of the wearer.*

White satin slipper, 1881

Roger Vivier shoe,
Winter 1963-64

Detail from 'Il a Eté Primé,' by J. Gojé,
*Gazette du bon ton*, 1914

Johnny Moke, 'Golden Ball' shoe, 1988

# THE JEWELLED SHOE

*Decorative deliciousness is a recurring theme in the history of women's shoes – sadly, it dropped out of men's fashions at the time of the French Revolution and has never returned except for some attempts to reinstate it in the 1960s and 1970s.*

*Women's shoes have rarely reached the heights of decorative confidence that is exhibited by surviving examples from the early eighteenth century. The exception is found in the creations of Roger Vivier. He has consistently and magnificently designed shoes that have all of the charm of eighteenth-century shoes but, in fact, show an even more fertile imagination. But Vivier's shoes are not mere copies or pastiches, as the decorative shoes of lesser designers can sometimes be. What makes them unique is the fact that, for all their ornamental extravagance, they are essentially modern designs. They could only be the products of this century – not least for their exploitation of the principles of engineering and aerodynamics. Where Vivier has led, other designers – Andrea Pfister, for one – have followed. The shoes on these pages are encouraging proof that deliciousness is still alive.*

*Above:* Shoe by Andrea Pfister, 1970s

*Above:* Shoe by Andrea Pfister, 1972

*Opposite:* Shoe by Roger Vivier, 1964

# BOWS AND POM-POMS

*Louis-Alexandre, Comte de Toulouse, caparisoned like a champion Shire at a horse show, appears to be rather pleased with himself in his knee-rosettes and grand shoes with large frilly bows. He is clearly confident that anyone of quality will be struck by the fact that he is wearing the last word in seventeenth-century high fashion.*

*Much the same smug self-satisfaction of the fashionable man can be detected in the face of the Earl of Dorset, whose shoes are embellished with the extravagant roses of ribbons that caused moralists to speak out against such costly self-indulgence. Rembrandt's portrait of Marten Soolmans, painted in 1634, shows an even more histrionic rose made of stiffened lace which almost engulfs the shoe. When a fashion has reached this level of exaggeration it is doomed because it has pushed its decorative impact to the limit and no more development is possible. Something new must appear in order to move fashion forward.*

*Although bows and pom-poms went out of fashion as symbols of male power and wealth, they have always remained popular with women, for whom they signify a mild sauciness more decorative than decadent. Andrea Pfister's black velvet evening shoes with bow trims are low on modesty and high on sexual dash.*

*Above left:* Rembrandt, *Marten Soolmans*, 1634

*Left:* William Larkin, *Richard Sackville, 3rd Earl of Dorset*, 1613

*Opposite page*
*Bottom left:* Etching by Etienne Drian, 1914

*Top:* Court shoe for Miss Rayne of France Collection, Spring and Summer 1964

*Centre: Louis-Alexandre, Comte de Toulouse*, anonymous, 2nd half 17th century

*Far right:* Sketch for a shoe by Andrea Pfister, 1988

# STATUS SHOES

For all but the most abjectly poor, shoes do a lot more than merely protect the feet. In fact, what they project is every bit as important as what they protect: and in many cases much more so. Certain shoe styles have the effect of conferring on their wearers membership of a club. They signal clearly who and what their wearer is and why he is different from (and superior to) the rest of mankind. As clearly as the red heels worn by Louis XIV and his courtiers bespoke nobility, so certain modern styles murmur money, class and privilege.

The most famous status shoe of the twentieth century is the Gucci loafer. In the last decade the green and red canvas ribbon caught by gilt horseshoe buckles has become synonymous with the sort of laid-back arrogance that considers swanky dressing the antithesis of style. Gucci loafers stand for the social confidence of the casually wealthy – though cheap copies and over-exposure have weakened the power of the message.

*Top:* Gucci crocodile oxford, 1988

*Above:* Gucci loafer, 1988

*Above: Louis XIV and His Heirs*, French school, c. 1715-20

*Left:* Ralph Lauren slipper, 1988

An even more exclusive sign of a certain style is the Ralph Lauren slipper with the gilt embroidered decorative motif. To own a pair of these is a real sign of ease with one's privileged social position as they are meant to be worn privately at home. In theory, at least, they are seen only by those in the know.

By deliberately not being easily accessible, Ralph Lauren's slipper might escape the fate of Britain's most commonly understood status symbol: the green wellington boot. Originally designed for the sort of feet that trod only the pavements around London's fashionable Sloane Square and the loam of the more socially acceptable English shires, it has now become the cliché of the masses.

Wellington boots by Hunter, 1988

# HEELS

*Playing decorative games with the heels of shoes was an indulgence of shoemakers even in the days when long sweeping gowns hid heels from view for most of the time. As feet and ankles have become progressively exposed in this century, it has become an obsession with designers to push the design of heels to the limits of practicality.*

*The great shoemen of the century, such as Perugia and Ferragamo, were always eager to experiment with new materials, shapes and textures and, in so doing, frequently evolved heel shapes of startling originality. Not always beautiful, they rarely failed to be arresting. Unfortunately, few of their more exciting ideas could be adapted for mass-production. They remain in the province of the 'one-off' designer shoe, created to a standard of quality regardless of cost.*

*Modern shoemakers have tried many ways of making the heel as light as possible. The development of new materials enabled them to make heels higher and slimmer than ever before and, by adapting engineering principles, they could even create a heel-less high-heeled shoe. The same lightness and transparency were achieved less expensively in the 1950s when see-through heels became a practical possibility on the mass-market level. These often had semi-precious stones and decorative devices caught in them and one memorable pair were filled with water in which swam live miniature goldfish.*

Handmade heel-less shoe for Delmanette, shown in American *Vogue*, 1959, photograph by Attie

Model for a sandal by Ferragamo, of gold kid with heel in
layers of brass forming a pyramid shape, 1930

Anonymous Portrait of a Lady,
1770

*Left:* Coil-heel shoe by
André Perugia, 1953

Suede shoes with solid silver filigree heels, 1958

# PLATFORM SOLES

*Time has not dealt kindly with platform soles. They almost always manage to look ugly and ridiculous, as they frequently were at the time. In this century there have been only three revivals of the platform sole. In the thirties they were often made of cork and were used with wedge heels to make casual sandals for the beach. In the forties they were made of wood and were a practical solution to the problem caused by the shortage of leather. But it was in the aberrant seventies that they became a full-blooded fashion, made and covered in virtually every material under the sun.*

*Left:* Elegant cyclists, Paris, June 1942

*Left:* Platform shoes by
Ravel, shown in British
*Vogue*, 1972, photograph
by Jouvelle

# THE BROGUE

Brogues have come a long way from the Irish footwear that gives them their name. Originally, a brogue was one of the simplest but most effective of the practical peasant styles, created with nothing more in mind than protecting the feet with the maximum efficiency. That is why they were made with holes in the skin: it seemed the easiest and quickest way to drain away the water that collected in the shoes as they forded the sodden Irish bogs.

The brogue crossed to England as footwear for gamekeepers and ghillies who needed a shoe that would withstand all weathers. Its success came to the attention of the squirearchy, who took it up as the ideally tough shoe for stalking and shooting.

Having climbed the social ladder, the brogue became refined. While losing none of its sturdiness, it grew increasingly elegant and was even considered suitable for ladies following country pursuits. Its apotheosis was reached in the 1930s when the world's arbiter of fashion, the Prince of Wales, wore it as a golfing shoe and, in a lighter form (and to the horror of clubmen everywhere), in suede with a grey lounge suit as suitable wear for town. With such a pedigree, it is not surprising that the brogue style has become a firmly established perennial fashion for men and women.

*Portrait of Edward VIII* by Sir William Orpen

Women's heeled brogues, 1930s

Men's brown calf
semi-brogue by
McAfee, 1988

Greta Garbo, *c.* 1930

Mahogany
'Renoir' brogue
by McAfee, 1988

# THE CLOG

The clog is one of civilization's most successful examples of design. As a simple, hard-wearing solution to the problem of clothing the feet of the poor and physically hardworking in a practical and inexpensive manner clogs are surely perfect. That is why their design and manufacture are the same today as they were six hundred years ago. There are two basic clog designs. The more ancient is nothing more sophisticated than a solid block of wood hollowed out to take the foot and shaped to follow its contours. The variation is the clog with the shaped wooden sole onto which is tacked an upper of virtually any material the maker cares to choose. It is normally of leather but it is frequently of plaited raffia. Clogs used in heavy industry can have uppers of rubber, heat-resistant plastic and even metal.

Although essentially working footwear, clogs have been worn over the centuries by any country dwellers who required warmth, comfort and mobility in miry lanes. During World War II governments encouraged people to turn to clogs as a practical solution to the dearth of traditional raw materials in the shoemaking industry. Fashion magazines patriotically photographed clogs worn by top models in an attempt to give their evident utilitarian values sufficient glamour to overcome the stigma of working-class poverty that many people thought they carried. Their efforts failed and even when the middle classes did wear clogs it was very much under duress.

*Left:* Detail from *Market Scene* by Pieter Aertsen (1508-75)

*Above left:* James Heywood, clog maker, Wigan, Lancashire, 1939. *Above right:* Fashionable British clogs, photographed during World War II

Unemployed miner, Wigan, Lancashire, 1939

Outskirts of Haarlem, Holland, 1940s

# WORKING SHOES

For the majority of the world's population, for most of the world's history, shoes have had little to do with power or glamour; they have primarily been armour in the battle with the hostile climates and terrains that man had to overcome in order to survive. As exercises in practical design, working boots and shoes are stripped down for function. Decorative details and fashion fripperies have no place. For that reason, there is a remarkable consistency in the appearance of the footwear of working men and women. The medieval farmworker would feel perfectly at home wearing the Edwardian labourer's boots; the sixteenth century pantry maid would feel totally at ease in the Victorian factory girl's clogs.

Even the upper classes opt for practicality on the few occasions when they must do physical work. Vita Sackville-West's gardening boots are beautiful not just because they are handmade, but also because their form so perfectly fits their function.

*Top:* Mr Hubert Clarke, Somerset farmer, photograph by Bert Hardy, 1956

*Left:* Cooperative dairy at Stege Church rural deanery on the Island of Mou, Denmark, *c.* 1889

*Opposite:* Vita Sackville-West's boots, photograph by Edwin Smith, 1962

# THE MALE BOOT

The paradox of boots is that although they are essentially practical items of clothing they have always been fashion articles for all but the lowliest peasant. Dandies, mashers, fops and Macaronis have never accepted that merely because boots are utilitarian they need be dull. Military men, yeoman farmers, gentlemen and horsemen have taken pride in them as objects that reflect their individual style, class and position in society.

Fine boots were important indicators of social status from before the sixteenth century until beyond World War I. Over the centuries their design gradually became less flamboyant but that did not reduce their importance. Sixteenth-century boots, as worn by the gentleman class, were extravagantly decorative. Made of exquisite leather, softly wrinkled, they were worn with their tops turned down. As the century progressed they became increasingly ornamental and were frequently topped off with lace or elaborately cut fine leather.

At the same time more practical boots, the forerunners of those worn in the eighteenth and nineteenth centuries, began to evolve. Essentially meant for serious riding, they were more rigid and protective and were often made of waxed leather for greater strength and style. In the early nineteenth century boots became increasingly divorced from the specialist gear of riding and took their place as normal daytime footwear for all smart and fashionable men-about-town. Hessians, wellingtons, top boots and dress boots were all made of the finest leathers.

As the nineteenth century continued, these calf-high boots were superseded by the much less flamboyant boots and spats which signify the tempered Victorian male's approach to dressing for vanity. Boots were never as flashy again until stage and film cowboys revived them. They continue today as pop stars' props in colours and skins that would have made the fastidious Beau Brummell faint clean away in horror.

*Top:* Portrait of Beau Brummell by Richard Dighton, 1895

*Left:* **Henry Rich, 1st Earl of Holland**, studio of Daniel Mytens, *c.* 1590-before 1648

*Left:* Tony Curtis

*Below: Incroyable* by Carle Vernet, Paris 1814

Courrèges boot,
1964-1965

*Above, right to left:* Meucci/Russell & Bromley (2), Charles Jourdan, The Chelsea Cobbler.
Photograph by David Bailey for *British Vogue*, 1971

*Left:* Blue cotton boot with white stripe,
English, mid-19th century. *Right:* Fawn
cotton boot with brown stripe and brown
leather toe caps, English, mid-19th century

132

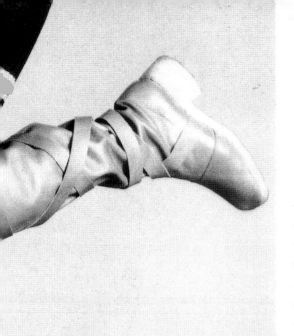

# THE FEMALE BOOT

*Boots for women have taken various forms over the last two hundred years. They have, by turns, been severely elegant, purely simple and unabashedly sexy. For an ostensibly utilitarian form of foot covering they have at times been remarkably decorative, but they are at their most aesthetically pleasing (as are all shoes) when their designers concentrate on line and forget applied decoration.*

*What could be more elegant and timeless than these ankle boots from the 1840s in understated ticking? They would be perfectly suitable for wear today – in fact they are the clear forerunners of the famous space-age boots introduced by Courrèges in the early 1960s. Even more akin to the space-age boots are the long narrow boots with squared-off toes and shiny leather trim that date from the 1850s. This remarkably forward-looking footwear anticipates the functional purity of modern aeroplane and motor car design in its streamlined elimination of all superfluous detail.*

Boots advertisement on a shopping bag from the London firm of Elliot, 1967

Boots, English, 1851

A WELLINGTON BOOT
or the Head of the Army

*Above:* Caricature of the Duke of Wellington. 'A Wellington Boot, or the Head of the Army'. Handcoloured etching by 'Paul Pry', 1827

*Right: Napoleon Crossing the Alps* by Jacques-Louis David, 1800

*Below:* Adolf Hitler inspecting the guard of honour at Nuremberg, September 1938

*Opposite:* Operation Starlite, Vietnam, 1965, photograph by Tim Page

*Inset:* Drying boots on the Swift Boat, Ca Mao Peninsula, Vietnam, 1969, photograph by Tim Page

# THE MILITARY BOOT

'A soldier in shoes is only a soldier', said General Paton, 'but in boots he becomes a warrior'. No matter how impressive they may look, however, boots that are not up to standard in battle are soon cast aside. Military boots are offshoots of the peasant's working boot. Made of the toughest leather and cut high to support the ankles, they are essentially tools of war. Wellington took the greatest pains to ensure that his armies were properly booted; other generals, including Napoleon, who did not always take the same personal interest, frequently had cause for regret.

There is a world of difference between the boots worn in Vietnam or Northern Ireland, whose efficiency might literally mean the difference between life and death, and the dress boot, worn to impress. Generals on parade want glamour boots, whether they are Napoleon painted as an icon of power or Hitler strutting before his guard of honour.

## *SHOWBUSINESS AND RECREATIONAL FOOTWEAR*

SIR EDWARD RAYNE joined his father's firm as a keen young man in 1940. One of his first tasks was to oversee the making of the shoes for a John Gielgud production of a Restoration comedy. Rayne was introduced to Gielgud at the dress rehearsal and he asked if the shoes were satisfactory. Gielgud's reply was withering: 'Mr Rayne, the day when the public is aware of my shoes is the day my theatrical career is over.' He was right. Stage shoes should be so well-judged for the character that they are not noticed. However, that does not mean that they are unimportant.

Studying a part and 'getting into' a character frequently begins with the feet, and many actors have admitted that knowing how a character walks is of vital importance. In *About Acting*, Peter Barkworth tells the story of Wendy Hiller taking tea at the Ritz with the men who hoped she would agree to play Queen Mary in the stage production of *Crown Matrimonial*. After much discussion of the role, Miss Hiller said, 'Yes, I would like to take this part because I know what her feet will be like.' Demonstrating the correct out-turning from the ankle, she looked down and said, 'Yes, there are her feet. These feet are royal.'

Hop-pickers dancing in a barn, September 1951, photograph by Bert Hardy

Despite the fact that audiences may be completely unaware of them, the attention to detail that makes a performance successful must always include thought about the shoes, even if it does not actually start with them. During the play, the actor should be able to forget all about them. Ill-fitting shoes are even more of a problem onstage than off. On the first night of Peter O'Toole's *MacBeth*, he tripped over his shoes and one of them shot off, giving him the job of replacing it without bending down. It says much for O'Toole's stage presence that he managed this, but at what cost to his confidence for the rest of the scene can only be imagined. Like all aspects of theatrical design, shoes are only successful if they work for the actors. Their reliability should be taken for granted, just as their style usually is.

It was not always the case. From the 1890s to the end of World War I, fashion followers took great interest in the shoes worn by the popular actresses of the day. Top shoemakers in Paris, New York and London designed their most avant-garde styles to be worn on the stage. Actresses could wear provocative colours, like scarlet, which was the theatrical rage of late Victorian times; extreme styles, such as the very high heels worn by the French music-hall star Mistinguett; and materials and jewelled decorations which would have been unacceptable in polite society. Even in their private lives actresses could get away with shoe styles which would have been considered unspeakably 'fast' on other women.

Many of the greatest leading ladies of the late nineteenth century insisted on the right to decide what they would wear on stage. Someone of the stature of Ellen Terry would employ her own dressmaker and *bottier* to create a costume suited more to her own status than to the needs of the character. No matter what part these *grandes dames* of the theatre were playing, they were always glamorously shod. After the performance, they slipped on bright satin shoes easily removed at dinner in case the current beau wished to drink champagne from them. Ruby Miller, one of the great music-hall stars, is reputedly the first woman to whom this happened. Her rival Ada Reeve let it be known that she felt it must have been a very disagreeable experience for the drinker.

Baudelaire described dancing as poetry with arms and legs. Just as poetry requires great efforts to appear effortless on the page, so does dancing. Early ballet was hardly more demanding than the courtly ritualistic dances from which it evolved. It was an aristocratic pastime performed by aristocrats. Although the shoes worn for ballet were often specially designed, they usually followed current court fashion. The only exceptions to this were shoes for characters which required a special costume, as Boreas did, for example, in Ben Jonson's *Masque of Beauty* – contemporary reports speak of his feet ending in serpents' tails.

If the King himself performed, his costume had to be heavily laden with symbolism. Jean Berain, Louis XIV's favourite designer of masques, created for his monarch's performance in the Royal Ballet of the Night a Sun-King costume that included high-heeled shoes with massive gilt sun buckles, complete with rays, which echoed the magnificently glittering motif of the whole outfit.

Extravagant courtly costumes were swept away by the French Revolution and, in the nineteenth century, increasingly technical demands made on dancers meant that shoes which were merely versions of those in ordinary wear would no longer do. The first modern ballet shoe was based on the 'straights' worn for ballroom dancing and had no blocking in the toe. The new form of dancing introduced in 1831 by Marie Taglioni in her performance in *La Sylphide* forced the

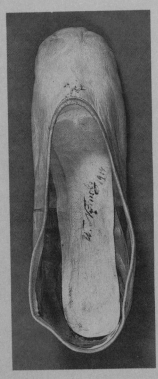

Cream leather ballet shoe
autographed by Nijinsky, 1914

invention of a strengthened toe. Taglioni danced on points, so creating modern ballet and, with it, the need for more robust shoes.

In 1862, Emma Livry, a ballerina at the Paris Opéra, burnt to death when her dress caught fire during rehearsals. Her ballet shoes survived. Unblocked, and strengthened solely by darning at the sides, they weighed only 34 grams each, whereas Pavlova's modern, blocked shoes weighed 74 grams. By the beginning of the twentieth century, dance had become so demanding that blocked shoes were essential. Early cotton wool padding had been replaced by toes stiffened with glue and darned for extra strength.

Specialist shoes demand specialist makers, and these appeared in every city that had a ballet company. In the eighteenth century, the Paris Opéra had been pre-eminent in Europe and it continued to be so for most of the nineteenth, so it is not surprising that the most successful shoemakers were found in Paris. The most famous were Janssen, who made Taglioni's shoes, and Crait, who founded his firm in Lyons in 1823. Crait moved to Paris in 1850 and his fame spread to such an extent that in the 1860s Adele Grantzan, the principal dancer in the St Petersburg ballet, started to order her shoes exclusively from him. In 1879 he was made official supplier to the Paris Opéra – an honour still held by the firm today.

Ebermann of Berlin, Romeo Niccolini of Milan, Capezio in New York, Gamba in London – the Belle Epoque saw the founding of many specialist ballet shoe firms. Capezio was opened in 1887 by Salvatore Capezio. The shop was opposite the Metropolitan Opera and Capezio moved into theatrical footwear by accident when Jean de Reske, who was performing in *Romeo and Juliet*, lost his shoes and asked Capezio to make a quick replacement pair. From then on, the firm came increasingly to specialize in ballet shoes. The London firm of Gamba was founded by Luigi Gamba, an Italian who had arrived in England penniless in 1894 to work as a waiter. By 1912, Gamba was designing for Pavlova and Nijinsky, as well as selling exotically coloured evening shoes, with turned-up toes *à la Schéhérazade*, to fashionable ladies. Other long-established ballet shoe makers include the London firms of Anello & Davide and Frederich Freed.

Modern performers use up shoes at a phenomenal rate. A major ballet company can easily go through three thousand pairs a year. Dancers are provided with one or more pairs of shoes a week and they usually look after their shoes themselves, darning them and attaching the ribbons. Although most dancers hate this chore, they do it because they alone know exactly where they need the strength. Ballet stars are very particular about their shoes. Natalia Makarova has said that out of ten pairs she might find only one that is comfortable. For a key performance, it was not unusual for Rudolf Nureyev to try on as many as six pairs in the wings before finding the right ones.

Not surprisingly for something as important and intimate as a shoe, dancers tend to have favourite suppliers. Patrick Buiell has worn Capezio shoes for most of his career; Anthony Dowell prefers Gamba. Whoever makes the shoes, the performing life of any pair is limited – often to one night. They literally shred and fall apart on the feet. Mikhail Baryshnikov recalls continuing in performances wearing shoes with split sides and separating soles, and his experience is not unusual.

Clog dancing is a form of dance often overlooked, but it was a popular working-class entertainment in England from mid-Victorian times to World War II. Just as ballet shoes, light and insubstantial, seem to reflect the aristocratic beginnings of the dance, so clogs, solid and hardwearing, convey the strength of

Red leather tap-dancing clog, *c*.1914

urban industrial cities. The point of clog-dancing is that the dancer creates his rhythm by tapping with his toes and heels. To make the dancing clog lighter than its work equivalent, the uppers were cut low at the ankle and a lightweight wood such as ash was used for the soles. Professional dancers were extremely nimble-footed and some could perform complex steps at great speed. They danced singly, usually on a square slab of slate or hardwearing wood that made a ringing sound when the clog struck it. Amateur dancers would introduce drama by nailing clog irons to their soles so that sparks flew during the dance.

Clog dancing was almost exclusively a male pastime. Although music-hall bills often included women, the purists watched only the men. Troupes of clog dancers were common in the north of England in the last decades of the nineteenth century. One of the most famous was J.W. Jackson's 'Eight Lancashire Lads'. Charlie Chaplin joined this troupe in 1896 and was paid £1 a week plus his keep. Towards the end of the nineteenth century clog dancing was introduced to America, where it was quickly transformed into tap dancing, which became a mania from coast to coast.

Clog dancing had been predominantly a male dance, and men also took to tap dancing. However, it was especially popular with women and chorus lines were soon tapping away in U.S. vaudeville theatres and London music halls for audiences equally as enthusiastic as those who were enjoying the cancan in Paris. The girls wore special shoes called mary-janes, kept on with an ankle strap fastened with a buckle or button. The shoes were often 'split clogs' with half the sole and the heel in wood. To emphasize the sound, some shoes had 'jingles' attached to the shank. When the heels hit the floor they made a sound like two coins struck together.

Ballet shoes, clogs and tap-dancing shoes were as specialist as the tight-rope walker's pumps and had little use in the everyday world. However, there has always been a need for shoes which are extraordinary without being specialist. We have already talked of the footwear of seventeenth-century masques, most of which could be worn, without giving rise to too much comment, for daily life in the court. The democratic development from the masque was the fancy-dress ball and the carnival. Dressing up has been a human pleasure for centuries and the masque was merely an exclusive and highly formalized version of it.

It was in the Belle Epoque that fancy dress became almost an obsession with the wealthy and privileged. William K. Vanderbilt's ball in 1883 in New York, or the Duchess of Devonshire's ball in London in 1897 cost the guests a fortune and kept the top couturiers busy. The desire for authenticity was so strong that even the shoes, though rarely seen, had to be modelled, at least loosely, on the correct wear of the period. In fact, it has been suggested that the popularity of classical goddesses and mythical figures as characters had much to do with the alluring golden sandals that were part of their costume. Certainly, Poiret's fantastic fancy-dress parties frequently had a Persian theme because the costumes and curling, pointed slippers lent so much scope for ingenuity.

The most popular male characters at fancy-dress balls were Louis XIV and Louis XVI – two monarchs who wore lavishly decorative shoes with high heels and bejewelled buckles far removed from the sombre footwear of the late nineteenth and early twentieth century. At one of the last great fancy-dress parties, held in Venice at Palazzo Labia in 1951, the host, Charles de Bestinqui, changed his costume six times during the long night. Each change had to fit with the shoes he wore throughout the party – sixteen-inch platform heels, no doubt chosen to add nobility to his 5 foot 6 inch stature.

The history of pantomime goes back to Harlequin in the Italian *commedia dell'arte*, who wore tiny black pumps in which to strike the formalized attitudes expressing admiration, flirtation, thought, defiance and determination. It was in the nineteenth century that pantomime recognizably similar to its modern version first appeared.

The glory of the panto is the principal boy, who is always played by a woman. James Agate stipulated that ideally the principal boy should convey the impression of having dined on tripe and onions and stout immediately before stepping onto the stage. He is meant to be a confident extrovert in thigh-high boots, but far too many modern principal boys are self-consciously glamorous and wear prim, high-heeled courts instead. In the 1870s the costume was almost a uniform: trunks, tights and such saucily laced boots that they made one of pantomime's earliest principal boys, Lydia Thompson, a sensation when she toured the U.S. Boot-blacks in Chicago subscribed to buy her a silver presentation wreath in gratitude for the fillip she had given to their trade.

Pantomime shoes are normally glamorous, but the men who play the grotesquely ugly women who are a major part of many pantomimes are shod as clumsily as possible in footwear that has traditionally been a parody of poor working-class boots – heavy and badly made. Patched and with soles coming adrift, they are meant to make Widow Twankee (a close relative of Charley's Aunt and Old Mother Hubbard) look coarse, though with a heart of gold for all that.

The Ugly Sisters in Cinderella are always dressed in a recently passed fashion pushed to ludicrously eccentric limits. Glamour is parodied as being very close to tattiness. Modern pantomime designers always make the sisters' attempts at sophistication appear grotesque, and they do this as much by the shoes as by make-up, hair or clothes. Almost always the shoes are based on the heavy platform soles and thick heels of the mid-seventies, a type that perfectly fits the idea of fashion gone wrong.

Chorus girls in pantomime have moved far away from the nineteenth-century corps de ballet, and this has given scope for exotic footwear. Silk and satin, covered with artificial pearls, rubies and emeralds, were used for Victorian chorus girls' sandals, but modern line-ups are more likely to be in the standard 'high-kicker's' high-heeled court with as many decorative additions as the designer can get away with. As in ballet, these shoes take a beating and need constant repair and renewal.

The circus ringmaster is the personification of male elegance in his black top hat, hunting-pink coat and white cravat. His boots are standard riding boots, made of fine black leather which is frequently patent and always immaculately clean. They are boots to show who is in charge. Unruffled and powerful, the circus master's image contrasts strongly with the chaotic, shambling disorder of the clowns. They are clearly out of control, as their clothes make clear.

Clowns have evolved standard types of costumes over the last century and, in so doing, have paid particular attention to their shoes. In every troupe at least one clown wears a pair of boots with ludicrously elongated flat toes. This exaggerated footwear has been part of the clown's costume since the early nineteenth century when Grimaldi wore shoes decorated with enormous rosettes. He was the first to adopt footwear which forced him to lift his knees in the clumsy, high-stepping

Cartoon of 'Little Tich', the originator of the clown's long shoes

One of a pair of clogs, 18 inches long, worn by 'The Whimsical Walker', 1860s-80s

stride that has become the trademark comic walk of clowns everywhere. Grimaldi frequently tied coal scuttles to his shoes to make his progress noisy and even more awkward. However, it was George Ralph, known professionally as 'Little Tich', who designed the long shoes which have since become the traditional footwear of the circus clown. Ralph was born with six toes on each foot, and must have started out with a broad, square-shaped shoe which he then elongated to the point of absurdity. He began his career in 1880 as a black-faced impersonator doing a big-boot dance and long boots soon became his signature. They were as long as he was tall but, despite the fact that they were almost like skis, he was able to dance on the toes without losing his balance.

The search for a costume that conveys a particular personality is basic to clowning and various clowns have found unique solutions. What they all have in common, however, is a form of footwear not in scale with the rest of the body. The trio of French clowns, the Fratellini brothers, always had one of their number dressed in shabby-genteel costume and shoes described as being like canal boats. Felix Adler, from Iowa, conceived a costume of extraordinarily padded proportions including bright yellow boots three sizes too large. The German clown, Karl Valentin, known as Munich's answer to Chaplin, was long and skinny. He emphasized his lankiness by wearing tights with boots like divers' flippers. In London, Thomas Dawson Walker, 'The Whimsical Walker', wore clogs that were eighteen inches long, but was outclassed by Coco the Clown, whose enormous boots extended twenty-five inches.

Clowns do not set out only to make us laugh. They also tap our sentimentality by engineering situations full of pathos. Early Hollywood stars like Buster Keaton and Charlie Chaplin did much the same thing. With both actors, the pathetic effect was achieved through the boots they wore, but it was Chaplin, the little man buffeted by forces beyond his control, who used his boots and distinctive walk to such telling effect. He treated his boots, misshapen, broken and elderly as they were, with the reverence and love of the peasant who knows that without them he is finished: no credibility, no mobility and, above all, no work. Chaplin's most moving scene was when starvation forced him to eat his boots, the only things that spelled hope.

In the late 1920s and 1930s, Hollywood became the dream machine, producing fantasy films highlighting the joys of the wealthy life – sophisticated drawing-room comedies were transplanted to Manhattan penthouses; soignée stars ate in chic restaurants and danced in smart nightclubs: it was a world far removed from the realities lived by the majority of cinema-goers.

Even more artificial were the spectacular musicals with 'casts of thousands' performing dance routines like automatons. These were the decades of the musical star. Singers like Nelson Eddie and Jeanette MacDonald were popular enough but it was the dancers who really drew the crowds. Fred Astaire and Ginger Rogers flashed across the screen in increasingly daring routines which broke the established pattern of dance roles. He was the star, she the supporting cast. His brilliant black patent shoes were featured much more prominently than her high-heeled dancing shoes. Where Fred Astaire established the beach-head, Gene Kelly, Donald O'Connor, the Jets and the Sharks and John Travolta all followed – the male dancers took the lead.

The male pop music scene has produced footwear ranging from the decorous Beatle boot to Adam Ant's piratical thigh boots. During the seventies, the high heels, platform soles, brilliant colours and exotic skins of the time were exploited by pop groups to the limits of their theatricality. Gary Glitter wore silver boots with three-inch platform soles; Elton John's built-up boots were such magnificently and deliberately camp extravaganzas that they were recently sold as works of pop art; David Bowie played different fantasies with each new album, but whether he was Aladin Sane or Ziggy Stardust his boots were always glamorous, high-heeled and platform-soled. The Bay City Rollers decorated their boots with tartan and Punk groups like the Clash wore ankle boots with zips and pointed toes.

In the late eighties, the fancy dress component in the footwear of pop groups has receded and its place has been taken by the ubiquitous street shoes: sneakers and trainers. These are now the signature footwear of casual and disengaged youth, for most of whom they have little to do with their origin as sportswear.

Rubber-soled footwear was developed in the United States in the middle of the nineteenth century. A patent was granted to Wait Webster of New York in 1832 for his process of attaching rubber soles to shoes and boots and by the 1860s the first kind of sneaker shoe with a laced canvas upper and a rubber sole was in production as a croquet sandal. This was followed by the Spalding Company's rubber-soled canvas tennis shoe. Exactly when the sneaker ceased to be exclusively a player's shoe and became a leisure shoe is not certain, but it had become accepted in the U.S. as casual wear for children by the turn of the century.

A parallel process was taking place in Great Britain. After unsuccessful experiments with cotton uppers and a variety of materials for soles, the New Liverpool Rubber Company developed a rubber-soled, canvas shoe of the same type as the earlier American one. Because the join between the two parts was sealed with a contrasting band of rubber similar to the line painted on ships to denote the safe loading level, introduced in 1876 by Samuel Plimsoll, the new shoes were nicknamed plimsolls – a name still current. Like their American counterpart, plimsolls were not confined to tennis courts and croquet lawns. They soon became standard beach wear and were commonly worn by children for outdoor play.

These were the earliest specifically designed sports shoes. Organized sport was largely a late-nineteenth-century invention and well into the 1880s cricket, football and rugby were commonly played in ordinary, hobnailed, heavy-duty leather workboots, which were unmodified except for the occasional addition of rows of metal studs to give greater grip. Twentieth-century sport has been characterized by the quest for increased performance. In the majority of sports, the improvement has been dependent on speed and this has forced the makers of sports shoes to produce lighter products. Modern rugby and football players would be exhausted if they had to play in the earliest sports boots. These protected the ankle and had a toe cap of specially strengthened leather and studs made of layers of leather. They weighed 500 grams when dry but could be twice as heavy in wet conditions. The modern boot is a streamlined design, cut low, soled in plastic and with screw-in studs. It weighs less than 250 grams.

The need for speed is paramount in track events and is obtained by reduced weight and efficient spikes. The first mention of a spiked running shoe occurs in 1852 and by 1894 the Spalding Company's catalogue featured three grades of spiked shoes. They were low cut, with kangaroo uppers, leather soles and six spikes. The top shoe in the range cost $6.00, a considerable sum at a time when the average American family of four lived on $11.00 per week.

The father of the modern running shoe was Adolf Dassler, who began making shoes in 1920. By 1936 his shoes were internationally acknowledged as the best and were worn by athletes of the calibre of Jesse Owens. To improve the strength of the shoe, Dassler added strips of leather to give support. His first 3-strip shoe appeared in 1949. It was the first modern running shoe, from which the trainer and the baseball boot evolved. In 1948 the Dassler business split and it was re-formed as two separate companies: Addas (later to be known as Adidas) and Puma. Both firms remain today in the forefront of the immense running shoe business.

The first running shoe based on sound orthopaedic principles, without seams and with a very wide foot base, was introduced by New Balance in 1962 to sell direct to athletes by mail order. The modern track shoe with its mesh fabric uppers and super-light synthetic soles can weigh less than 96 grams. It is as aerodynamically efficient as Concorde and quite as beautiful.

Shoes and boots of man-made materials have proved to be efficient and reliable. Not only are they light, they also have the advantage of being more easily mass-produced than boots made in traditional materials. As sport has become faster and more aggressive, the need for safety has increased – man-made materials allow safeguards to be incorporated in the design. The change to synthetics has revolutionized specialist sports footwear like the ski boot and has also made possible completely new forms such as the underwater swimmer's flipper. The world-wide obsession with sport and its effects on ordinary footwear have already been discussed, but it is highly likely that in the next decade sport will be the catalyst for all clothes design and our present trainers and sneakers will be seen as only the first tentative moves towards making the fashion world one enormous international sports stadium.

Ballet shoes at the Royal Academy of Dance, London, 1988

# BALLET SHOES

Our modern idea of classical ballet dress is based on the costume worn by Marie Taglioni when she danced the title role in La Sylphide at the Paris Opéra in 1832. A lithograph of her in the role shows her poised on points although at this stage in the development of the ballet slipper the toes were still unblocked and were merely darned for strength. Even in 1862 the ballet shoes of Emma Livry were still not blocked in the modern way. Like all early point shoes, they were stuffed with cotton wool padding to take the strain of the dancer's weight. By the mid-1860s shoes of the kind worn by the corps de ballet painted by Degas were stiffened with glue as well as being darned in order to give them the necessary strength. The design of ballet shoes has not changed: Taglioni could slip into Martine Van Hamel's with total ease and the only thing that would surprise her would be the degree of comfort that the modern slipper affords.

*Above:* Shoes belonging to the American ballet dancer Martine Van Hamel, 1988, photograph by Daniel Sorine

*Left:* Marie Taglioni in *La Sylphide*, 1832, lithograph after Chalon

*The Ballet Rehearsal* by Edgar Degas, 1878-79

# BALLET IN FASHION

Ballet shoes are the simplest of all forms of footwear. Their flexibility and ease of movement have appealed to women for almost two hundred years. The elegant woman dancing at a public ball in 1803 wears heelless slippers exactly equivalent to the ballet pump of the period. In the 1940s Claire McCardell asked Capezio, New York's top manufacturer of ballet shoes, to make her flat pumps suitable for the streets – and they have been popular ever since.

The plain black pumps shown by Norma Kamali in 1989 demonstrate that their simplicity still makes pumps the most elegant of shoe styles.

Costume de Bal, from *Costume Parisien*, 1818

Pumps by Dolcis, British *Vogue*, 1954, photograph by Cecil Beaton

*Opposite:* Pumps by Norma Kamali, 1989

# TREADING THE BOARDS

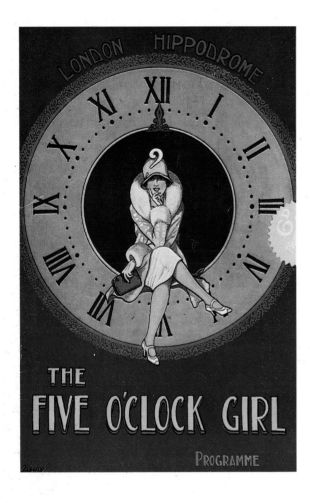

Poster for *The Five O'Clock Girl*, October 1930, London Hippodrome

In music hall, vaudeville and pantomime the demands made on footwear are different. Colourful, practical footwear for quick, lively movement, including dancing, leaves little opportunity for fantasy or originality. A style once proved to work tends quickly to become established as a tool for the job. A classic example of this is found in the circus, where the long clown's boots devised in the nineteenth century by Little Tich are still standard wear in any circus in the world.

The influence of the theatre on the design of shoes has been slight. In fact, most theatrical productions in the past gave them scant thought. The designer of an historical play often made do with a vague approximation to the style of the period. In contemporary plays the shoes were almost always versions of currently fashionable styles.

During the 1980s things have changed and costume designers are now as determined to get footwear correct as they are at pains to ensure that every other item of clothing is in period. They are right to be so because even when the actor's feet cannot be seen the shoes he is wearing are of enormous importance in the creation of the part. Many of the world's greatest theatrical figures have admitted that when they are 'thinking' themselves into a character they begin with the shoes, because these will dictate the way in which the character will stand, move and generally fill the part.

Postcard advertising *The Bohemian Girl* by Batfe, *c.* 1905

Poster for Le Cirque sans Bluff, c. 1930

# DANCING SHOES

'Aye, Aye, Aye, Aye, Aye, I love you
ver-r-ry much,' sang Carmen Miranda in
her musicals during the 1940s. The
sentiment was reciprocated by her public
who flocked to the cinema to enjoy her
uniquely extrovert way of putting over a
song.

    Her audiences were also thrilled by
her over-the-top costumes which brought
bad taste to the level of a minor art form.
Her towering fruit and vegetable head-
dresses were unlike anything previously
seen but the most interesting aspect of the
'South American Bombshell's'
appearance was possibly her shoes. She
and her designers went back to the chopine
of the sixteenth century as a device to give
the diminutive singer the height to balance
the headgear and avoid a top-heavy
appearance. They were brilliantly
successful: Carmen Miranda's
appearance was unique. Fred Astaire, on
the other hand, was content merely to be
the greatest movie dancer of all time and
stuck to patent leather, traditional shoes
for his dance routines.

Fred Astaire

Carmen Miranda, 1940s

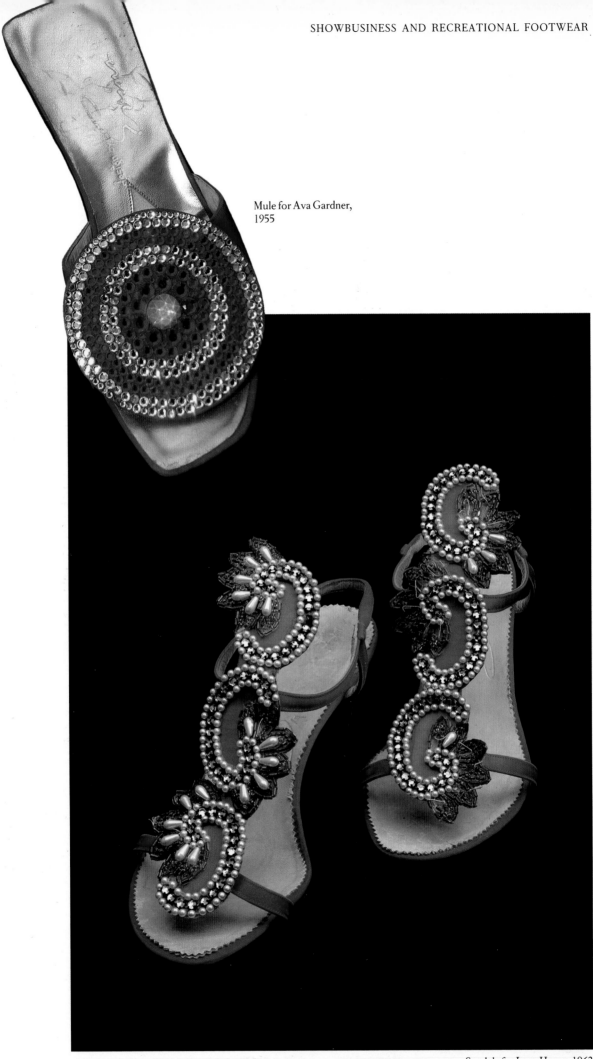

Mule for Ava Gardner,
1955

Sandals for Lena Horne, 1962

# STAR PERFORMERS

*Designing for the stars has always had a special appeal for shoemen. It is easy to see why. Film stars are frequently larger-than-life characters and they appreciate the value of extravagance. It is because they are used to projecting their personalities that they find acceptable (on and off screen) styles that less sophisticated women might shun.*

*David Evins has been a favourite of the stars for many years because he has the ability to create a shoe that reflects the character in the film while at the same time respecting the personality of the actress. He has worked with most of Hollywood's top movie actresses and has dressed their feet for some of the greatest box-office successes.*

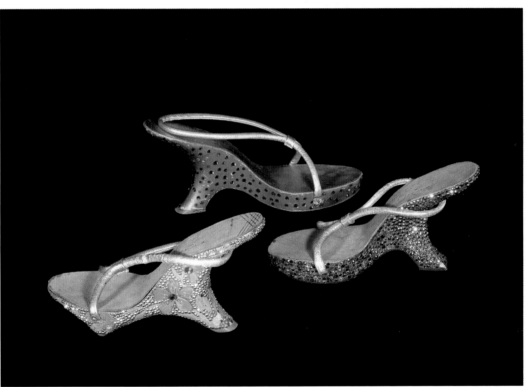

Sandals for Elizabeth Taylor in *Cleopatra*, 1963

Sandals for Elizabeth Taylor in *Cleopatra*, 1963

# COUNTRY DANCES

Footwear for dancing is usually unique. Over the years, shapes have evolved which are specifically designed to the purposes and needs of the performer. Not all performance shoes are so specialized and, as these pictures show, sturdy everyday footwear adapted for athletic dancers need not be graceless. There is elegance in the strength of the studded clogs of the coconut dancers from Bacup, Lancashire, England, who perform their ancient dances every Easter Saturday. Gleamingly clean, these shoes are business-like without sacrificing style.

 The coconut dancers wear a modified version of the working clog but the Bucharest Ensemble perform their vigorous routines in boots which could be worn on the streets without causing a second glance. The Portuguese dancers are similarly shod in non-specialized footwear. The grace and strength of Scottish Highland dancing are reflected in its traditional footwear. The heel-less pump is similar to a ballet slipper but it is laced and thonged like a ghillie.

*Top:* Portuguese dancers

*Above:* Scottish highland dancing

*Opposite:* Bacup dancers from Lancashire, England

*Opposite, inset:* Bucharest Ensemble

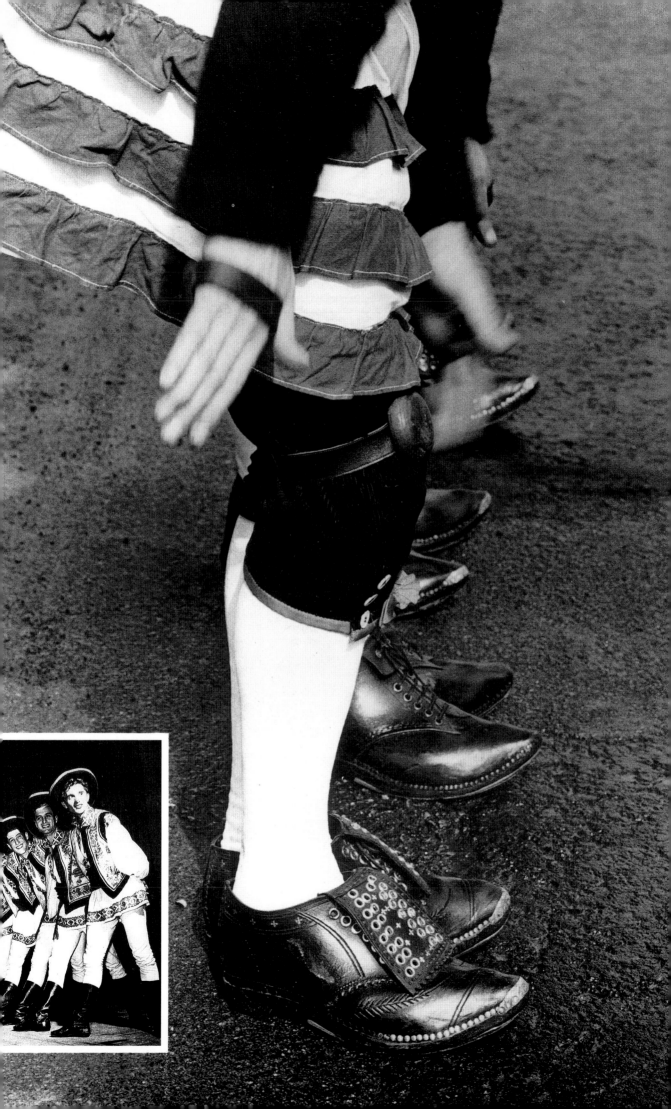

John Travolta in *Saturday Night Fever*, 1977

# FROM STREET TO STARDOM

*Things were never the same after* Saturday Night Fever, *starring John Travolta and Karen Gorney. For the first time in Hollywood musicals ordinary shoes worn on the streets were given star status. Travolta's white suit was the equivalent of King Arthur's shining armour: dress suitable for a hero and an icon. But Travolta came from the ranks of the kids and it was essential that he should not be totally deified. As a pop hero, he could only succeed if the kids on the streets still identified with him. That is where his two-tone shoes came in. Although wearing a white suit could cause a lot of trouble in the downtown scene, anybody could wear the Travolta dancing shoes – and did.*

Grease, *again starring Travolta, this time with Olivia Newton-John, took the movement towards making the hero accessible on to the next stage. There was no attempt to lead fashion or create a new style. The stars wore what their peer group were already wearing. Newton-John danced in 'middle America' high-heeled sandals of the kind which college girls had been dancing in since the fifties, and Travolta wore the oxford style of the same era. Baseball boots were the other fashion that took centre stage in the Travolta films.*

*These styles were certainly not new; what was new was that a film star with Travolta's charisma could make it 'Hip To Be Square'.*

John Travolta and Olivia Newton-John in *Grease*, 1978

# BROTHEL CREEPERS

*It was Elvis Presley who gave young people the confidence which enabled the salesmen of the world to create in the 1950s a new sub-culture: the teenager. With his 'Blue Suede Shoes', a mocking celebration of the obsession with looks that was one of the cornerstones of the 'youth quake', he gained the support of young and old alike – not to mention the shoe manufacturers of the world.*

*Presley's audience included the young male exemplified at his peacock heights by the Teddy boy, spawned in the United States but given an identity in London. Teddy-boy clothes soon became a uniform, as all successful male fashion always does. The long, draped jacket, the skintight drainpipe trousers and the baroque hairstyle gave him a strongly individual appearance, but what caught the imagination of the public was his shoes. Almost always suede (pace Elvis), they usually had enormously thick soles which earned them the affectionate name of brothel creepers. Their semiotic language was translated in the late seventies into the twin tongues of Doc Martens and bovver boots.*

British Teddy-boys, 1970s

British Teddy-boys, 1950s

# JAZZ HARMONIES

In the early 1920s jazz moved across the social barriers that had divided black and white music and it suddenly became chic to dance to the sounds of Bix Beiderbecke and King Creole. The effect on fashion was considerable. 'Jazz styles' were the thing in New York, and even in Paris the sporty looks introduced by Chanel and Patou reflected the mood of the times.

One of the most popular fashions for both sexes was the two-tone shoe, introduced in the twenties but at the height of its popularity during the thirties. Like the new music that brought together blacks and whites, the co-respondent shoe (known in the U.S. as the spectator) echoed the surface mood of musical racial harmony. It was black and white or brown and white and was equally popular with people of both shades – provided that they had the elegance and style to carry it off. Although essentially a 'sharp' style, and most popular with show-business extroverts, it had a long run as the very smoothest sort of golf shoe. Its connection with the Prince of Wales is well known, as is Fred Astaire's fondness for it. Here he and Gene Kelly are dressed in the height of Hollywood suavity: white double-breasted suits, boaters and immaculate spectator shoes, looking like absolute twenties' mashers. As the Bally shoe from 1989 shows, the two-tone shoe is a style that has a following regardless of what is happening in fashion.

Gene Kelly and Fred Astaire in *Ziegfeld Follies*, 1946

*Right:* Advertisement for 'Lifestride' shoes, from Brown Company, USA

Two-tone shoe by Bally, Spring/Summer 1989

British dance hall, 1940s

# ANARCHY SHOES

The urge to decorate items of clothing with political slogans and symbols began in the early 1960s and was another side of the flower-power hand-painted decoration on clothes that made the hippy movement so colourful. The fashion spread during the sixties and seventies, stimulated in particular by the anti-Vietnam War movement and by increased political activity by students in Europe and the United States.

    These anarchy shoes, designed by Dirk Bikkembergs, testify that it is still fashionable to wear your political opinions on your clothes. They make their statement by taking the knee-jerk words of the eighties and crudely scrawling them across the surface of the shoe. 'Hard Rock Café', 'Sex Pistols' and 'Suicide' make these shoes suitable only for the more extrovert of young anarchists . . .

'Anarchy Shoes', designed by Dirk Bikkembergs, 1988/89

# PUNK AND POP

Much of the potency of pop singers stems from their appearance. How they dress is almost as important as how they perform; in fact, their clothes are part of the performance.

Madonna's message is a complex one that works on several different levels. Her tight patent leather shoes in this picture conjure up associations of dominance, which are reinforced by the rest of her costume.

Michael Jackson, the superstar of the late eighties' pop scene, has chosen ordinary loafers, perhaps to soften the perverse message of the rest of his costume.

The most successful pop star when it comes to creating a bizarre appearance must be Elton John. As the pinball wizard in Tommy, he wore the largest and most magnificent Doc Martens in the world.

Groups like the Sex Pistols and the Damned showed their alienation by wearing black leather festooned with zips and safety pins, as well as studded belts and wristlets and heavy toed boots. Jan Jansen's male and female Punk boots have the trappings but lack the aggression – this is a designer approach to anarchy.

Elton John in *Tommy*, 1975

Jan Jansen's Punk shoes with steel caps, 1977

*Opposite page*
Michael Jackson in concert, 1988

*Inset:* Madonna, Wembley Stadium, London, 18 August 1987

# SNEAKERS

The sneaker is the most powerful and lasting shoe design of the twentieth century. Quite apart from its strength as a design in its own right, it is of great importance as the precursor of the training shoe which is perhaps second only to the clog as the universally democratic footwear worn by people of all ages and nationalities.

The word 'sneaker' was first used in 1875 and it referred to the early croquet shoe which had been developed in the United States using the newly invented vulcanizing process to make rubber soles for the white canvas uppers. The sneaker went through many design modifications before becoming a popular teenage fashion in the late 1950s. Symbols of rebellious youth, such as James Dean, and pop stars like Buddy Holly gave sneakers a sexual quality that made their lure even stronger. Possibly because they were inexpensive in virtually every country, they soon became the universal footwear of the burgeoning student classes.

In Jailhouse Rock, Elvis Presley was followed by very young fans of both sexes, all wearing sneakers, saddle shoes (their close relation) or loafers – which were in their turn to become a world fashion, symbolizing middle-class, Ivy League attitudes.

Sneakers were not only socially OK, they were artistically acceptable and, inevitably, began to appear in pop art works. Claes Oldenburg, whose artistic reputation rests on his ability to take ordinary and even banal artefacts from everyday life and, by changing their scale and placing them in unexpected (and even ostensibly inappropriate) places, make us see them in a new light, naturally turned his attention to the sneaker. He saw it as the lasting symbol of the great American contribution to world culture: casual, egalitarian and accessible. Whether future generations will agree with him is arguable but his enormous sculpted gym shoe will certainly bring home to them the other aspect of pop art: its droll sense of humour.

Elvis Presley in *Jailhouse Rock*, 1957

Daley Thompson, Olympic Decathlon Champion, 1984

# FOOTBALL FOOTWEAR

*Football boots have undergone surprisingly few design changes in the last seventy years. Most of the modifications to the original design have been stylistic and have largely taken place over the last ten years as the game has become increasingly glamourized.*

*Oddly, for such an avidly followed sport, soccer has had virtually no cross-over influence on everyday shoe design, though Dirk Bikkembergs' Summer 1987 Collection clearly reflects the detailing and lacing of professional boots.*

*Top:* Young footballers at Pooles Park School, London, late 1930s

*Above:* Dirk Bikkembergs shoes, Summer 1987

*Opposite page:*
*Top left:* Dirk Bikkembergs shoe, Summer 1987

*Left:* Football match between Queen's Park Rangers and Nottingham Forest, England, 1988

# SEASIDE SHOES

Beach shoes were, to use an expression in vogue at the time, all the rage in Victorian times and remained so up to the 1930s. They were essentially disposable items; if they lasted a season they had done well. Their function was to save the wearer's street shoes from the effects of salt water and sand. Few Victorian bathers, who were only just becoming familiar with the pleasures of seaside holidays, would dream of going down to the shore without the protection afforded by beach shoes – a protection against moral degradation as much as against unknown terrors from the deep.

Mack Sennett's famous bathing belles were not normally seen in his films in the twenties because the censors were nervous that the young men in the audience might become dangerously aroused by the sight of so much flesh. Sennett included them in his film schedule so that line-ups like this one could be snipped out of the film and used for publicity in newspapers and magazines. Part of their undoubted sex-appeal lay in their beach boots which are an out-of-doors adaptation of the standard chorus girl's boot of the day.

Bathing dress, from *Harper's Bazaar*, 1876

*Below:* The Sennett Girls, early 1920s

# THE DESIGNER AND THE DEVELOPMENT OF STYLE

**S**OME WOULD CLAIM that modern fashion began in 1858, the year Charles Frederick Worth opened his couture house in the rue de la Paix. Up to this time, dressmakers and man milliners had been tradespeople, subject to the whims of their customers and inclined to do no more than deprecatingly attempt to interpret their wishes. Worth was the first modern couturier – that is, a man who created his own designs and then offered them to customers.

Although a fundamental and daring shift in power, this move was spectacularly successful. In a few years, Worth was the arbiter of Paris fashion. Women begged and wept to be allowed to buy from him, abrogating all authority over their appearance, and only too happy to wear whatever he proposed. Most importantly, they were prepared to pay more for one Worth creation than they would have given an old-style dressmaker for an entire year's garments.

Wealth is power, and by the 1880s Worth's word was important not only in terms of fashion, but in all matters of taste. By the time of his death in 1895, the house of Worth supplied gowns to every royal house in Europe, including secret, unlabelled consignments to the court of St James.

Page from American *Vogue*, 1909, the first editorial shoe pictures ever to appear in *Vogue*

The success of the firm continued after his death because Worth, a shrewd businessman, had trained his sons Gaston and Jean Philippe to carry on. Jean Philippe was in charge of design and soon realized that his father's approach to clothes, which had so successfully captured the moods of the last decades of the nineteenth century, was less well fitted to the attitudes emerging at the beginning of the twentieth. In an attempt to bring the Worth salon up to date, he engaged in 1900 a twenty-one-year-old designer recommended by his friend the couturier Doucet. Paul Poiret – extravagant, lordly and brilliantly original – worked at Worth for four years, before leaving to set up his own house. It became an instant success. The famous Parisian actress Réjane, who was one of the city's leading fashionable figures, began to be seen in Poiret creations and where she led everyone followed. All Paris was soon talking about the young designer and his extraordinarily avant-garde designs.

In the period up to World War I, Paris was a city which lived for fashion. Appearance was not merely an adjunct to personality, it *was* the personality. The major fashion influence was exerted by actresses and *grandes horizontales* who spent a fortune (not normally their own) on the correct toilette. Fashionable designers had proliferated in Worth's wake and Poiret was joining a galaxy of talent unknown in any other capital. Doucet, Chéruit and Paquin all had their following and their workrooms were kept busy fulfilling the orders for the vast number of gowns which a life in high society demanded. The shoemaker as designer had yet to come into his own and most of the laced boots worn with the magnificent gowns of the period were made by the thousands of little *bottier* establishments found in every section of Paris.

Many of the shoemen worked anonymously to the orders of couturiers like Poiret, but the majority served their customers just as the dressmakers had done before Worth changed the rules. The *bottiers* were skilled at handwork, understood the demands of the fashionable temperament and worked quickly. A pair of shoes for an important occasion could be delivered within the week. However, not all bootmakers were simple artisans working under the guidance of the customer. Some, like Monsieur Ferry of rue de la Grange Battelière and Monsieur Chapelle in rue Richelieu, were already beginning to make their mark as shoe designers: men who originated styles and created fashionable footwear for the women who patronized the *grands couturiers*.

One of the most fashionable was Pinet. The son of a provincial shoemaker, Pinet was born in 1817 and learned the trade from his father. He arrived in Paris and set up his establishment in 1855, just at the time when Worth was beginning to tire of his subservient role at one of Paris's most fashionable drapers and was thinking of setting up on his own. Pinet quickly flourished as the shoemaker to the smart set. By 1861 he had won the Nantes Prize and in 1863 he opened an elegant establishment in rue Paradis Poissonière. Pinet's business expanded in the first years of the new century, though he himself had retired by then and his son had taken over. Pinet shops were opened in Nice and London. The firm's reputation was based largely on the Pinet heel, a much thinner and less splayed-out version of the rather squat louis heel. Fashionable women wore Pinet shoes well into the 1930s.

Fashion works on two quite distinct levels. Contemporary couturiers, milliners and shoemakers are pursued by followers of fashion because they are already well-known designers fashionable in themselves. Wearing a famous label is a sufficient achievement for most fashion followers. Such people exist in their millions and are constantly stimulated by fashion magazines to buy the products of the well-known designers whose advertisements keep such magazines in business. They are the reactors to fashion, not the initiators.

However, there is another sort of dedicated fashion follower, numbered only in the hundreds. They are the truffle hunters of style who unearth the riches, keep them a closely guarded secret as long as possible and only reluctantly hand them over to fame. This coterie of informed and dedicated fashion people demands a level of dedication and discernment which precludes all but the most obsessed. That is why, when women were flocking in their thousands to *bottiers* like Pinet, the shoemaker who was the genius of the age had only twenty customers – although it must be said that such limited numbers were imposed by him. His name was Yanturni and he was not a commercial shoemaker at all. He was an amateur enthusiast.

Yanturni was the curator of the Cluny Museum and made shoes only in his spare time. He had neither workshop nor assistants. Little of his life is known except that he was born in Calabria in 1890 of East Indian stock. How he came to Paris and what kind of life he led there are obscure and, in a sense, unimportant. What matters is that he made shoes so exquisitely flattering that women who could afford to buy wherever they wished would buy from no one but him. They were prepared to pay the considerable sum of $1000 down payment in advance, and in return Yanturni agreed to make their shoes for life – at his speed and in his numbers. A customer was quite happy to wait for over three years for delivery. When Yanturni had accepted a client, he made a plaster cast of her feet and on these he moulded his creations without necessarily seeing the client ever again.

Yanturni's shoes were treasured by the lucky few because they were light and delicate as cobwebs and made of extraordinary antique materials which he bought at flea markets or from collectors and fitted to each customer's personality. A piece of old brocade might immediately suggest one of his customers to him; he would buy it and make the shoe – often without consulting its eventual owner.

Yanturni's devoted clients included Nancy Lancaster and the amazing Mrs Rita de Acosta Lydig, a millionairess who literally spent her whole life and considerable resources in the pursuit of style. As a fashion purist, she was attracted to Yanturni's creative attitude and he in turn admired her perfectionist approach to the important subject of dress. The shoes he made for her were exquisite exercises in atavism. Using medieval velvets and cloth of gold, he crafted square-heeled shoes with toes pointed or straight; or, taking silver tissue and lace appliqué, fashioned evening slippers fit for a Renaissance princess. He did not stop there. Mrs Lydig bought up antique violins so that Yanturni could use their wood to make shoe trees that weighed only ounces. To further preserve these rare shoes, she had special trunks made for her in St Petersburg. Of Russian leather, and lined in cream velvet, they travelled with her wherever she went.

Yanturni was unique, and, despite the fact that he fully understood the art of shoemaking, he could not be called a shoe designer in the accepted sense of the term. The first of this century's great shoe designers was André Perugia. Born at the end of last century of an Italian father and French mother, Perugia opened his own shoe shop in his home town of Nice when he was only sixteen. He had left his father's shoe business after a demanding apprenticeship because he had become impatient with an approach to shoemaking where all thought went into making and none into the design. Like thousands of provincial shoemakers, Perugia's father made more or less the same shoe all his life. Perugia was much more interested in style and recognized that Nice was fashionable enough to provide a market for well-designed footwear with a touch of originality.

Perugia claimed to have been lucky all his life and, certainly, his luck started early in his career – helped, perhaps, by his looks. He was handsome and even in later life, when he was happily married, spent much of his time fending off the advances of customers. He dressed impeccably, held his spare figure erect, and always wore black and white spectator shoes and a straw hat.

One of his early clients was the wife of the proprietor of the fashionable Negresco hotel on the promenade. She took a great interest in Perugia and persuaded her husband to allow the young shoemaker to place a showcase in the hotel foyer. Perugia decided that in order to be talked about he must charge what was, for Nice, an exorbitant price. As he said later, 'If my shoes really pleased them, the women who went to places of that kind could just as well pay five thousand francs as five hundred.'

One of the first customers to come to Perugia's shop as a result of the hotel showcase was a woman who, he recalls, 'was so well kept that not one gentleman but a number were necessary'. She bought her clothes from Poiret, who was at this time at the height of his powers. Poiret soon noticed her fine shoes from the young shoemaker and despite his position as the most aristocratic couturier in Paris he was sufficiently excited to travel to Nice to invite Perugia to show his shoes in his dress house. But it was 1914 and the war prevented Perugia from taking up the opportunity. It was not until 1920 that he opened his establishment in Faubourg Saint Honoré to provide shoes not only for Poiret but for many of the other *grands couturiers* as well.

Apart from these collections, Perugia designed shoes for individuals and he particularly attracted a social and theatrical clientele. He designed for Mistinguett, the French music-hall star with legendary legs, for the Duchess of Penaranda, a fashion leader for whom he created a series of satin slippers with Spanish spike heels, and for Pola Negri, one of Hollywood's earliest stars.

Perugia's shoes were chic in an entirely Gallic way. He understood the engineering of a shoe but was at the same time able to catch in his creations the essence of Paris – 'the capital of all the elegances', as Edith Wharton described it. Behind the two or three attention-grabbing shoes that he created each season to ensure press coverage lay a solid body of exquisitely made footwear which showed Perugia to be one of the century's greatest shoe designers, if not the greatest. The bulk of his time was spent in making superb practical shoes, and it was with these that he began in 1927 his long association with the United States. In the interwar years he worked with Saks Fifth Avenue, as well as providing shoes for the English firm of H & M Rayne.

Between the wars, Perugia was considered the god of the shoe trade. He made shoes for everyone, including Queen Elizabeth when she made her state visit to Paris in 1936. He moved his premises to the fashionable rue de la Paix and he and his wife lived there in great style. During the twenties, Perugia had begun to collect Post-Impressionist paintings, especially those by his friends Vuillard and Bonnard. They hung in the flat where he entertained Paris's beau monde.

Perugia remained in Paris during World War II and throughout the Occupation he continued making shoes. Many of his customers were German officers. His popularity slipped after the war, but he went on working with the top couturiers,

including new designers such as Jacques Fath and Hubert de Givenchy, as well as creating collections for his international clients, who now included I. Miller and Charles Jourdan.

Drawings from the *Gazette du bon ton*, showing shoes by Perugia, 1920s

Perugia's place in the pantheon of shoe designers is a secure one. Although it was his fantasy shoes that brought him publicity and made him world famous – the slippers with heels of twisted metal or gold balls, the 1931 fish shoe inspired by Braque, the sandals based on paintings by Léger and Matisse – women who understood design bought his shoes because of their poise. Perfectly balanced and carefully scaled, they had the same visual and tactile appeal as a sculpture by Brancusi.

André Perugia was not the only 1930s shoemaker with an international reputation. Coming up fast was an Italian, Salvatore Ferragamo. Ferragamo differed from Perugia in that he was a ceaseless technical experimenter whose innovative approach was fed by a seemingly inexhaustible imagination. Many of his one-off designs have become twentieth-century classics whose wit and style save them from being merely kitsch.

Born in poverty in 1898 in the south of Italy, Ferragamo emigrated to the United States in 1914 at the age of sixteen. He was already a qualified shoemaker and, after settling in Santa Barbara, began making shoes for the American Film Company. In 1923 he moved to Hollywood, where he created shoes for biblical epics such as Cecil B. de Milles's *The Ten Commandments* and *The King of Kings*. Soon he was working for all the top studios, making shoes for John Barrymore, Lillian Gish and Rudolph Valentino, among others.

Ferragamo shoes were not only in demand for the screen. Beginning with Mary Pickford and her sister Lottie, he made increasingly for the stars to wear off-duty and also built up a following of wealthy individual customers. Ferragamo returned to Italy in 1929, but his firm went bankrupt in 1933. However, persistence and hard work enabled him to reverse his fortunes and by the end of the thirties his business was again thriving. Even in the thirties, Ferragamo was known for his innovative approach, but the privations of World War II, especially the embargo on the use of leather for non-essential items of footwear, further stimulated his imagination. He employed cellophane, fishskin and canvas for the cork-soled shoes and sandals that were a continuation of his earlier experiments. When the good quality steel which he had been using to strengthen the shanks of his shoes was commandeered for the 1936 Abyssinian War, he devised cork wedge heels. These were at first rejected by the public, but Ferragamo persisted and the wedge style eventually became the most popular shoe fashion of the war years.

Ferragamo's great days as a shoe designer came after the war. By a canny mixture of showmanship and sheer design panache, he ensured that his shoes were permanently in the news. The early fifties were halcyon days in Italy. Film production had started in Cinecitta, tourism was returning, Italian style was emerging. The stars and personalities flocked in. Portofino, the Costa Amalfitana and Rome were the places to be seen, but everyone took time to go to Florence in order to buy a pair of Ferragamo shoes. He measured the feet of virtually all the front-page personalities of the world, from Greta Garbo, who bought seventy pairs of shoes on one trip, to the Duchess of Windsor, for whom he made an annual spring order of spectator courts.

Despite the wild originality of many of his one-off shoes, Ferragamo always insisted that he was not a fashion instigator but a disciplined craftsman working within fashion's current boundaries. It is perhaps for this reason that he won the Neiman Marcus Award for design in 1947 (which his daughter Fiamma won exactly twenty years later) and, at the time of his death in 1960, had retail stores in most of the major cities of the world. His shoes always had character, and were frequently extravagant. The Maharani of Cooch Behar ordered one hundred pairs and sent real pearls and diamonds from India for decoration. Ferragamo's most outrageous creations were for Eva Peron, who insisted that he use the rarest skins and was happy to pay prices which even Ferragamo admitted were astronomical.

Ferragamo was a great showman, but he was also an extremely good shoemaker. The quality of his shoes rested on his understanding of the human foot. It was that understanding which enabled him to temper his fantasies with the need for comfort and ensured his success at both bespoke and mass market level.

Ferragamo laced shoe in black antelope, with prow toe, 1930-35

A good shoe designer requires artistic and scientific skills – his shoes must look and feel right. The balance between comfort and beauty is not always easy to achieve but when it is right the shoe will be as ergonomically satisfying as a suspension bridge and as delicate as an orchid. Roger Vivier is the designer who has most consistently achieved this balance. His creations combine visual deliciousness with mechanical precision in a way that exemplifies his belief that successful shoe construction depends upon harmony of form.

Vivier was born in 1913. An orphan, he was brought up in Paris by an aunt. He enrolled in the Ecole des Beaux-Arts to study sculpture, but left when he was nineteen in order to design shoes for his friends. Although he did not complete the course, what he learned at the Beaux-Arts was the foundation on which he built his shoe designing career.

Vivier creates shapes which have the strength of a sculptor's armature. Having got the basic engineering right, he can then play on any number of fantastically decorative ideas without weakening the structure. To look at a Vivier shoe is to see the clean lines of Concorde and the Rococo richness of the Amalienburg combined in a creation which has not sacrificed comfort for beauty.

Vivier had established his name before World War II and was creating shoes for Pinet, Bally, Rayne, Miller and Delman by 1939 – the year in which he designed a cork-soled platform shoe which was rejected by Delman but taken up with delight by the Italian couturier Elsa Schiaparelli, who was renowned for her Surrealist approach to fashion. Frustrated by the lack of materials during the war, Vivier channelled his creativity into millinery and had a great success in partnership with Suzanne Remi, with whom he opened a boutique on Madison Avenue called Suzanne and Roger.

After the war, Vivier returned to France and in 1953 began a collaboration with Christian Dior. He made bespoke shoes for the couturier's *haute couture* collection, followed by a mass-produced collection with Vivier's name on the label next to Dior's. This was the first time that a shoemaker had been given equal billing with a couturier.

Vivier shoe in green brocade with rounded toe and Regency heel, 1963-64

The two men worked together for the next ten years. The shoes were manufactured in France, England and the U.S. and Vivier's influence was disseminated worldwide, with considerable benefit to other designers and manufacturers. His 'comma' heel, square toe and *choc* heel, slanting away from the arch, were copied everywhere. His trims – sequins, ribbons, buckles and bows – instantly set fashion trends and his extravagant use of colours and materials broke through the barriers between mass-produced and custom-made shoes. Vivier's influence during these years was entirely benign.

When Vivier opened his own house on rue François Premier in 1963, he began to produce a collection under his own name, in addition to those he was already doing for Grès, St Laurent, Chanel, Ungaro, Balmain and Laroche. His customer list – a roll-call of the world's most fashionable figures – included the Duchess of Windsor and Marlene Dietrich. One of his most perceptive customers was *Vogue*'s Diana Vreeland, who has worn his shoes for the last thirty years and is reputed to have her maid polish their soles and bone the leather uppers with a rhinoceros horn. Vreeland believes that no one in the history of shoemaking has ever made soles better than Vivier's and describes them as being 'flat as tongues'. Sir Edward Rayne, after a lifetime in the shoe industry, says of Vivier, 'I have never known anyone greater,' a judgment with which most fashion experts would agree.

If Vivier is the king of the decorative shoe, Manolo Blahnik is undoubtedly the dauphin. His shoes are theatrical fantasies of the most extravagant kind, completely original combinations of wit, sex and allure. Like Vivier, Blahnik has the ability to take the spirit of a Georgian slipper or a Regency pump and re-create it in modern terms. He is no plagiarist. His works are no more copies of the past than were Vivier's decorative shoes for Dior. They are original creations of the moment, entirely contemporary and yet catching the Romantic spirit of previous ages.

To turn period thinking into modern design is dangerous to attempt and difficult to achieve. Historicism is popular with many young designers of the present day. Stimulated by the elegance of styles of previous centuries, they model their designs on them. What they produce with depressing frequency is a pastiche – at best a good copy of an outmoded style, at worst a bastard which is neither of the past nor of the present. A copy of an eighteenth-century shoe is a piece of nonsense at the end of the twentieth century, but a reinterpretation of the spirit of Georgian grace can be totally contemporary. The one is costume, the other is fashion. It is because Blahnik never confuses the two that he can bring off daring feats of historical legerdemain without a second's faltering.

Manolo Blahnik's background explains his cultural breadth. He was born in 1940 in the Canary Isles. His father was Czech and his mother Spanish. He was educated in Geneva, where he studied literature and art before moving to Paris in 1968. His introduction to the world of shoe design came in 1971 when he was visiting New York. He moved to London and by 1978 had become an established shoe designer. He is now the most influential shoemaker in the world and his tiny shop in Chelsea is visited by *jeunesse dorée*, film star and wealthy socialite alike. Blahnik's life is the peripatetic one of the internationally successful designer. He commutes between Italy, England and the United States but, totally in character, he chooses to live in Georgian Bath.

# THE MASTERS: PERUGIA

The greatest French bottier *between the wars was André Perugia. Famous for the wit and originality of his creations, Perugia was every bit as glamorous as any of his shoes. Tall and elegant, he was a heart-throb and rumour has it that at least two fashionable ladies threatened suicide because he refused to requite their love. He lived at the grandest level and an invitation to his apartment above his premises in the rue de la Paix was never refused.*

*Perugia made shoes for every woman who was anyone in Paris between the wars, including Mistinguett and the legendary fashion original, the Spanish Duchess of Penaranda. He also designed the shoes for the collections of Poiret and Schiaparelli, both of whom were completely in accord with his determination to create shoes that were full of fantasy but could still be worn with an elegant toilette. It is no exaggeration to say that Perugia was the only shoemaker for a woman of sophistication to patronize in the thirties and he worked with clients so dedicated to perfection that no thought of money or time could deflect them from the pursuit of excellence.*

*Opposite:* Perugia styles, 1930-35

Boots by Perugia for Schiaparelli, British *Vogue*, 1939, illustrated by Jean Pagès

*Above:* Sandal, 1940

*Above right:* Sandal, 1935-38

*Right:* Publicity sketch by Lucio Venna, 1930

The story of Salvatore Ferragamo's life is every bit as colourful and fantastic as the shoes he designed. Born in poverty in the south of Italy, he emigrated to the United States in 1914, aged sixteen. His rags-to-riches story began when he moved to California and began to design for the stars. His shoes very soon became their favourites, on and off the screen. He returned to Italy and set himself up in Florence in the early thirties but soon fell on hard times. By 1933 he was bankrupt but the determination that had originally taken him to America to make his fortune surfaced once again and in a comparatively brief time he had made a remarkable recovery. He never looked back.

Ferragamo came to the peak of his power in the late forties and early fifties. His witty, original approach to design made him a favourite with extrovert film stars like Paulette Goddard and Gloria Swanson; his understanding of the needs of the foot appealed to dancers like Alicia Markova and Katherine Dunham while his sheer newsworthiness attracted any woman who could afford his shoes, including most of the crowned heads of Europe, whether deposed or not.

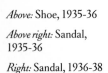

*Above:* Shoe, 1935-36

*Above right:* Sandal, 1935-36

*Right:* Sandal, 1936-38

# THE MASTERS: VIVIER

*Many fashion experts would claim that Roger Vivier has created the most beautiful shoes of the twentieth century – and it would be difficult to contradict them. His work in the fifties with Christian Dior marked a highpoint of the shoemaker's art. Light-hearted and extravagantly decorative, the shoes he designed at that time had the elegance that only a French designer achieves.*

*Vivier is the Fragonard of the shoe. Whereas in other hands his highly decorative approach could easily have become saccharine sweet and vulgar, his perfect taste*

*ensured that he avoided the pitfall. The other great skill that marked Vivier out from many shoemakers working at the same time or since was his unerring sense of knowing when to stop, the rigorous self-editing that is the hallmark of the great designer. And Roger Vivier is, without doubt, not merely a great shoemaker, but one of the great designers of the century. He alone of all the shoemakers is worthy of sharing the* victor ludorum's *plinth with Cristobal Balenciaga as the twin eminences of the twentieth-century fashion world.*

*Top:* Shoe by Vivier, 1963

*Above:* Shoe by Vivier, 1987

*Left:* Shoe for the coronation of Queen Elizabeth II, 1953

*Opposite:* Roger Vivier, 1988

# THE MASTERS: CLERGERIE

Robert Clergerie successfully combines the aesthetic requirements of the creator with the seriousness of the businessman. He believes that he must thank his early training with the French firm of Charles Jourdan for the fact that he is able to look after both sides of the shoemaking trade with equal skill.

Clergerie is a guru figure for many young designers because his designs are clean, simple and forward-looking. The uninitiated could be forgiven for assuming, on the evidence of his shoes, that the designer was in his twenties. In fact, he is in his fifties and his designs are fresh and modern because everything he does is a reflection of his belief that the simpler an idea is the stronger it will be.

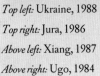

*Top left:* Ukraine, 1988
*Top right:* Jura, 1986
*Above left:* Xiang, 1987
*Above right:* Ugo, 1984

The type of customer who buys shoes at Blahnik would almost certainly have been a client of David Evins from the forties through to the early seventies. Dubbed 'The King of Pumps', Evins was the favourite designer of the stars, the wealthy and the powerful, all of whom recognized that he was a master of his craft.

Now in his seventies, Evins was born in England but emigrated to America when he was thirteen. After studying illustration at Pratt Institute in New York, he obtained a job as an illustrator for a footwear trade magazine. From here he moved more directly into the trade by producing style sketches and prototypes to sell to shoe manufacturers. In the early forties, Evins went into partnership with the firm of I. Miller to produce shoe collections under his own name.

The shoe style most associated with Evins is the basic pump. Stripped of extraneous detail, it has sold in its millions over the past thirty years. Evins keeps the decorative aspect of his mass-produced shoes severely under control but in his bespoke creations for actresses and women in public life he allows his imagination free rein.

One of his first 'hit' designs was a Carmen Miranda-style wedge clog made in alligator. Its theatricality made it a shoe for extroverts. It was a forerunner of the Evins style. His shoes have always been glamorous and his designs for show business personalities are elegantly glitzy.

There is hardly a performer for whom Evins has not created shoes. His list includes Elizabeth Taylor, Lena Horne and also Grace Kelly, for whose wedding to Prince Rainier of Monaco Evins designed a pair of low-heeled shoes in an attempt to minimize the height of the bride. He is a favourite of Nancy Reagan, for whom he twice designed shoes for wear at the Presidential Inauguration Ceremony, and he produces collections for New York's most sophisticated dress designers, including Geoffrey Beene, Bill Blass and Oscar de la Renta. Evins is without doubt his country's top shoe designer.

The same could be said of Maud Frizon in France. For the past twenty years she has been creating such original and innovative shoes that they have been described as being to footwear what Dom Perignon is to champagne. The Frizon company is jointly owned and run by Maud Frizon and her husband, Gigi De Marco. Frizon's background was in fashion. For several seasons, she had worked as a model for Patou, Courrèges and Dior. She began her company in 1979 by opening a tiny boutique on the Left Bank in the rue des Saints Pères. Her first success was a high boot that did not require a zip. Everyone in Paris wanted it – from fashion models to Catharine Deneuve and Brigitte Bardot. The zipperless boot put the new company at the centre of fashionable Paris, where it has remained.

Maud Frizon's quality as a shoemaker can be judged by the fact that she has created shoes for designers such as Azzedine Alaïa, Sonia Rykiel and Claude Montana. Her success as a businesswoman can be gauged by the fact that her firm produces more than a quarter of a million pairs of shoes per year – to be sold by two hundred retail clients throughout the world.

Frizon's approach to design is oblique. She rarely sketches because she believes that designing on paper cannot create volume and dimension. Nor does she cut leather. She believes that true design takes place in the factory with the craftsman and she works closely with her collaborator in her Italian factory before modifying designs to create new styles. It is a practical approach which has produced shoes of originality and wit. If shoes can be said to have a personality, none have more than the products of Maud Frizon's imagination. But her shoes, like

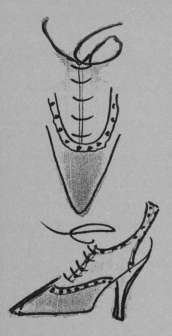

Sketches for shoe by Maud
Frizon for Spring 1989

those of the designers already discussed, are not merely exercises in design embellishments: they work because she understands the architecture of a shoe.

Women shoe designers have, until recently, been fairly rare and, with the exception of Frizon, have worked in America. Two of the earliest in the field were Nancy Knox and Beth Levine. Like David Evins, they both worked with the manufacturer I. Miller. Knox was with the firm in the fifties, but went independent in the seventies with such success that she received a Coty Award for her men's shoes. Beth Levine was at I. Miller in the late forties; when she married Herbert Levine in 1950, they set up a joint company.

Beth Levine was an innovative designer, prepared to experiment with unexpected materials – she used bamboo for making heels – and her husband was an excellent salesman. The firm flourished and Beth Levine won a Neiman Marcus Award and a Coty Award for her contribution to the shoe trade. Many of her theories of shoe design are based on the practicality, elegance and comfort of the American Indian's moccasin and her workmanlike approach is summed up in her essentially practical dictum that 'it is the shank and shape of a last which determine heel height and the pitch of the heel which determines the balance of the shoe. Get those right and you've got everything right.' Although Beth and Herbert Levine's company no longer exists, her influence in the American shoe business is still felt.

Joan Halpern has an unusual background for a shoe designer. She met her husband, David, when she was doing a postgraduate degree in psychology at Harvard; he was Chairman of the Suburban Shoe Stores. They married in 1968 and went into business together, setting up their company under the name Joan and David.

Joan Halpern recalls that in common with the vast majority of shoe designers she is largely self-taught. She learned the rudiments of the business by working for a small shoe concern in Boston before she and her husband formed their company. Joan and David is based in Italy and the Halperns spend half the year in Tuscany. Their firm is big in the way that manufacturers who are also retailers do grow big, and can be compared with Ferragamo, Jourdan and Frizon. Joan Halpern's designs are aimed at the sort of international woman she describes herself as – 'always running through airports' – for whom she can produce sensibly laced leather classics or frivolously jeweled pumps. Her success in doing so has been acknowledged by a Coty Award.

Susan Bennis, an American, and Warren Edwards, an Englishman, have worked together since 1972. They also have no formal design training and became shoe designers because the shoes they wished to sell in their New York shop were simply not available. Their first collection in 1973 consisted of ten styles. The shoes were manufactured in Italy – as they still are – and, from a small beginning, Bennis and Edwards now have a design studio on 57th Street and a Park Avenue shop.

Shoe design is like sculpture, painting or tailoring. Just as an expert would never confuse a sculpture by Hepworth with one by Moore, a painting by Johns with one by Rauschenberg, or an evening dress by Christian Lacroix with one by Geoffrey Beene, so a Blahnik bow could not be taken for one by Vivier, or a Perugia heel for a Ferragamo. It is not merely the trim which differentiates them, though that is distinctive enough. It is the designer's touch which creates a shape impossible to confuse with that of anyone else. A shoe designer's handwriting is as distinctive as that of any other creator and, although it will evolve and take in the newest developments in fashion, once established, it will not change. Experts could easily pick out an early and late shoe by one designer from a sea of others simply because of his touch – though the styles might be entirely different.

Pfister, Clergerie and Jansen are European designers of whom this is clearly the case. All have an originality and style which makes their work instantly recognizable. Andrea Pfister is of Swiss stock and yet his shoes seem so essentially Italian that it is no surprise that he studied in Milan and spends a great deal of his time in Positano – surely one of Italy's most colourful of fantasies – as well as living in Northern Italy.

Pfister is first and foremost a colourist. He is also one of the wittiest of shoe designers: his light-hearted sandals which push the parameters of good taste to their uttermost limits cannot fail to raise a smile. It is no surprise that he creates shoes for Mariuccia Mandelli, one of Italy's top dress designers, whose Krizia clothes often show a sense of humour. Light, frivolous and inconsequential as Pfister's contribution to shoe design may seem, he is a true original.

Quite as ebullient as Pfister is the Dutch designer Jan Jansen. Jansen's career began in 1964, when he worked under the name of Jeannot, but the two thousand shoe designs which he has produced since then reflect a spirit of anarchy more in tune with the seventies. Most of Jansen's shoes are an affront to good taste but, as he has said, they evoke a 'visual irritation' which is pleasing. They are so extreme in concept, colour and shape that one could be forgiven for thinking that he works only in one-offs for museums. On the contrary, Jansen is a practical, commercial shoemaker and expects his popular models to sell in hundreds of thousands. In common with all great originals, he has problems with plagiarists and has frequently been forced to invoke the law to prevent pirate versions of his shoes. Like Ferragamo, with whom the forty-three-year-old Dutchman shares an obsession with the wedge heel, Jansen makes handmade shoes to order as well as producing designs for ready-to-wear quantity production.

Pfister and Jansen are the entertainers of the shoe world. Robert Clergerie is its aesthete. At fifty-five he has been described as being as simple and balanced as the shoes he creates and this is perhaps why he has had such a considerable influence on other designers. Rigour has always characterized Clergerie's approach. After a peripatetic life he joined the Charles Jourdan organization in Romans to run a subsidiary of the firm. That was in 1971 and it was ten years later that Clergerie founded his own company. Its success is testimony to his managerial and administrative abilities as well as to his skill at judging what the public is ready for in design terms. His approach to design is simple: the stronger the idea, the less the need for decoration. He could be called the functionalist of shoe fashion.

People like Joan and David Halpern, Maud Frizon and Robert Clergerie are business men and women as well as creative shoemakers. In fact, as in all areas of design, the more successful a designer becomes, the less time he spends creatively and the more he is preoccupied with finance and business. All successful designers are forced to employ teams of young designers who work anonymously under their guidance. In some cases, the individual designer will create the main 'story' of the season and leave his team to multiply it with variations in order to make a complete collection. In others, the team might be given no more than a verbal briefing, or might even have carte blanche to come up with a wide range of ideas from which the designer will make a selection. However it is achieved, the design for shoes for a large company is not usually the sole work of one man in the way that the work of a *bottier* like Manolo Blahnik clearly is.

The blurring of the identity between businessman and creator is the penalty paid for large-scale success. Some of the most influential businesses in this century were founded by men who were primarily interested in commerce and saw good design only as a means of generating it.

At the turn of the century, there were shoe manufacturing companies enough in Europe and the United States but they were usually producing cheap footwear at a competitive price and often of low-grade materials. There was a gap in the market between these companies and the exclusive bespoke shoemakers, a gap that was peopled by the newly confident middle classes who wished to be well-shod without the discomforts of mass-manufactured products or the cost of made-to-measure. In the decades up to World War II companies grew steadily to serve this market and in the 1950s they burgeoned into worldwide, multi-million-dollar businesses.

Bally in Switzerland, Charles Jourdan in France, H & M Rayne in England and Delman and I. Miller in the U.S. have been continuing catalysts to the shoe trade throughout the century. They have initiated new techniques, employed top designers and, because they have had the money to advertise, have made the public increasingly conscious of fashion footwear.

American and European approaches to big business differed even as early as the end of the last century. U.S. shoe manufacturers were much more open to new ideas but, more importantly, they were serving a large and egalitarian market. Their products did not merely have to please the poor; they were bought by the middle and even upper classes. As a result, the importance of fit was recognized as an essential part of the designing process long before European mass-marketing firms gave it much priority. The difference between a ready-to-wear fashion shoe from the U.S. and one from Europe in the 1920s was considerable. The American shoe was not only more stylish and more comfortable; it was available in a range of sizes, colours and materials unheard of in Europe. The American equation was: technical excellence plus design ability plus money for investment plus a demanding customer equals thriving, forward-looking businesses.

In the first decades of the twentieth century, the U.S. shoe industry benefitted enormously from the influx of immigrants from Europe, especially Italy. It is interesting that Italy did not produce manufacturing giants in the shoe business early this century as other European countries did. They had no equivalents to Bally or Jourdan until well beyond the fifties. The reason is two-fold. Italy was slow to develop a demanding middle class of any significant size and Italian craftsmen had left in huge numbers for America. That is why the American companies leapt so far ahead. Not only was there money and the demand to encourage expansion, but in the Italian immigrants they could tap a level of creative skill way ahead of anything available in Europe at the time. It is commonly conceded that the best shoe craftsmen are Italian and that is why Italian design has led the world in ready-to-wear shoe manufacture since the fifties. What is not so readily understood is that in the twenties the U.S. was the Italy of the shoe world and its pre-eminence was largely based on the skills of Italian immigrant craftsmen.

One of the most important U.S. manufacturers was I. Miller, a New York based company founded in 1880. Israel Miller had arrived from Russia via France and, after working for some time in the shoe business, opened his own establishment on 23rd Street, specializing in shoes for the theatre.

At this time, women's footwear was almost exclusively in the form of boots, so shoes were a novelty and the shop attracted women who preferred them.

I. Miller shared with Capezio a monopoly as shoe supplier for Broadway productions: his shop was advertised as 'the Show Folk's Shoe Place'. From 23rd
Street, shoes went to all the theatrical celebrities, including Ethel Barrymore, Mary
Pickford, the Dolly Sisters and Bill 'Bojangles' Robinson. By the time of Miller's
death in 1929, the firm was known coast to coast and had a well-established policy
of employing the best designers to create collections for it. Perugia had been the
first of many and he collaborated with I. Miller for over thirty years, during which
time the firm became famous throughout the world for the high quality of its design
and manufacture.

By the thirties, I. Miller had moved away from theatrical shoes and was
making and retailing fashion shoes for the upper end of the market. Their standards
became so high that I. Miller products have been described as the best shoes in the
world during the thirties and forties.

I. Miller was not the only firm manufacturing fashion shoes to retail through
its own outlets at this time. Herman Delman, one of the most extrovert characters
of the shoe world, had a shop on Madison Avenue and was known as a producer of
high-class, expensive lines. Delman was always the showman and did things in the
grandest manner. At heart a retailer, he understood the importance of publicity:
Delman was the first to use film stars in advertisements and to design shops with an
aura of theatrical glamour.

Peep-toed ankle-strap sandal
by Delman/Rayne, 1950

Delman, who came from Portland, Oregon, was one of the earliest shoe
manufacturers to take on the big retailers and insist that his name appear on the
label. Many retailers bought anonymously and then put their own labels in the
shoes – as, of course, they still do today. Delman believed that quality shoes should
be attributable to the manufacturer and he is reputed to have once torn up a sizable
order because the buyer refused to feature his name. No such problems sullied his
relationship with Saks, where Delman had a highly successful shop-within-a-store,
or his partnership with Bergdorf Goodman, which began in the late thirties and
which Delman built up into the highest class shoe business in New York.

The heyday of the U.S. fashion shoe industry was the period from the mid-
thirties to the early fifties. Americans wore exclusively home-produced shoes;
there was no competition from other countries and firms were able to expand at
great speed and to an enormous extent. However, after World War II the American
shoe industry became a victim of its own success. Over-expansion and high costs
forced manufacturers to sell out to large conglomerates and by the mid-seventies
all the great names in shoe fashion were bankrupt.

Peep-toed wedge shoe in tartan
by Delman/Rayne, 1950

The multi-million dollar retailing giant Genesco bought both I. Miller and
Bally at one stage. Delman, who had opened a London shop with the English shoe
company Rayne as far back as 1937, sold out to Genesco in the late fifties and this
vast company put Edward Rayne in charge of the Delman division. In 1961,
Genesco sold half the Delman business to Rayne on condition that he would run it
and, for the next ten years, Rayne-Delman shoes were highly successful, selling
more than a billion and a half pairs annually. In 1973, Genesco sold Rayne-Delman
to the English firm of Debenhams.

H & M Rayne has much in common with I. Miller. The firm was founded in
1886; the founders, Henry and Mary Rayne, had met in Glasgow; he was Irish, she
Scottish. Anti-Irish feeling persuaded Henry Ryan, as he was properly called, to
change his name to Rayne before moving to London, where the couple set up as
theatrical costumiers in the Waterloo Road. At this point, shoes were merely a part

of the business. From the 1890s until after World War II, Rayne provided costumes and stage make-up as well as ballet shoes and theatrical footwear. Apart from Gamba, Rayne were overwhelmingly the specialists in theatrical shoes, as I. Miller were in New York. In fact, just as the programmes of Broadway productions almost invariably read 'Shoes by I. Miller', so those in the West End had, for decades, read 'Cigarettes by Abdullah, Shoes by Rayne'.

Rayne's ballet shoes were worn by Pavlova (who was featured in the firm's advertisements), Nijinsky and all the members of the Ballets Russes. But working with theatrical companies, though exciting, was not without problems, the main one being that such companies constantly went bankrupt. Rayne decided that the theatrical business was proving too risky and that it would be expedient for the firm to concentrate on shoes.

Initially, the firm's major customers were actresses and prostitutes, but the New Bond Street shop slowly began to attract a grander clientele and in the mid-1930s Queen Mary granted Rayne a royal warrant. It was the first of many. Rayne have provided shoes for three generations of British queens and a high proportion of princesses.

The Continental equivalents of Rayne, Miller and Delman were Bally of Switzerland and Charles Jourdan in France. Both firms became hugely successful in the 1950s and currently account for a considerable proportion of world sales. Carl Franz Bally started making shoes in 1851 but sales in Switzerland were poor and he saved his company only by starting to export to South America in 1854. From this uncertain beginning grew a firm of world stature which became a joint stock company in 1907. Bally opened factories in Lyons, France, in 1913 and Norwich, England, in 1933. The 1950s was a period of great expansion: several new factories were opened to service a worldwide network of Bally shoe shops.

Charles Jourdan was set up in Romans in 1929 and after World War II the founder's three sons joined the firm. René looked after the administration; Charles, jr, was in charge of manufacture and Roland was responsible for design and production.

It was Roland who made Charles Jourdan shoes the best in the world during the fifties and sixties and who increased sales in the following decades with a highly imaginative and challenging series of advertisements photographed by Guy Bourdin. Roland Jourdan has been described as 'overwhelmingly the most able man to emerge in the shoe industry'.

'Maxime', 1958 *(top)* and 'Madly', 1972 *(above)*, two of Charles Jourdan's most popular styles

There is no country that can compete with Italy in sheer volume of first-class designers. Italy is a tribal country and good designers usually gather their family around them to form a dynasty. The founder very quickly becomes a businessman but he keeps a watchful eye on the design level and ensures that standards are maintained. This dual excellence in both business and design is an almost exclusively Italian phenomenon. In other countries, the financial aspects of the firm are looked after by accountants who do not interest themselves in artistic matters; in Italy, the money-men admire and respect the designers – and frequently have been designers themselves. That is why the best mass-produced shoes are now all Italian.

Mario Valentino – who left his father's firm in Naples to design for films and became famous for his shoes for Ava Gardner in *The Barefoot Contessa*; Vittorio Pollini – whose business empire is founded on the fact that he makes the best boots in Italy; Renzo Rossetti of Fratelli Rossetti – whose skill as a designer of men's

shoes has successfully translated into the women's market; Natalino Pancaldi –
who has expanded the business founded by his grandfather in 1888 and exports to
every country in the Western world; Guido Pasquali – who made his name in the
1960s with glitzy shoes for Rome's dolce vita set and who still specializes in
theatrical styles; the list of top Italian shoemakers is as impressive as it is long.
They have developed the traditional artisan skills of the local shoemaker and
placed them firmly on the world stage.

It is the craftsmanship of the artisan that has inspired the newest wave of shoe
designers. The young creators who are producing shoes with a strongly romantic
or theatrical sense of style tend to be clustered in London, though they are not all
British. Designers specializing in shoes made to high standards of craftsmanship,
frequently by hand, working alone in studios or with a small band of assistants, are
a manifestation of the mid-eighties fashion strength of England. Young fashion
designers like John Galliano and Rifat Ozbek have focused attention on London in
the way that Katherine Hamnett and Vivienne Westwood did at the beginning of
the decade. Shoe designers are in London because they wish to benefit from the
buzz of design excitement, and also because they like the proximity of Paris, where
designers of the originality of Jean-Paul Gaultier are working. It would be too
formal to call the new London shoe designers a school, but they do have much in
common, including in many cases a desire to reshape the past which frequently
makes their designs look like museum pieces.

Best known and, in commercial terms, most successful is Emma Hope, whose
popularity is based on a romantic perspective best summed up in her own words
when she described her shoes as 'regalia for feet'. Her shoes feature softly sculpted
detail and any one of them could be worn in a Restoration drama without looking at
all out of place. Patrick Cox is a Canadian who designs shoes with a harder edge to
them. He has a feeling for anarchy and iconoclasm and has worked with Body Map,
Vivienne Westwood and Galliano, all of whom have attempted to ruffle the feathers of the bourgeoisie. Other young designers of note are Jimmy Choo, Elizabeth
Stuart-Smith, Christine Ahrens and Trevor Hill.

Python-skin platform court
shoe by Christine Ahrens, 1988

Johnny Moke is forty-four and has had considerable experience in fashion as a retailer and designer. He began designing shoes ten years ago and his forte was the outlandishly witty statement based on clever juxtapositioning of contrasting fabrics and finishes and bizarre decorative devices. In the eighties, he came under the romantic influence and is at present designing classic shoes which have a touch of fantasy. Although not one of the London designers, Dirk Bikkenbergs, who is based in Amsterdam, has much in common with some of London's post-punk creators.

The twentieth century has seen fashion develop with increasing momentum. In the shoe business, designers and manufacturers have brought about change at an unprecedented speed and volume. Some of the most important advances in shoe design, however, have been stimulated not by shoemen but by couturiers and dress designers who have treated shoes as part of an overall fashion look.

Until the 1950s, shoe design and the design of clothes were kept entirely separate and there was interplay between them only at the level of couture. With the burgeoning of ready-to-wear in both fields, this situation changed, to the great advantage of shoe design. Even so, major dress designers often create more forward-looking shoe fashions than those of the shoemen: Chanel's sling-back pump is a good example of a design so in tune with women's needs that it becomes a classic; Balenciaga produced a widely popular fashion when he sent the first thigh-high boots down the catwalk; Courrèges's space-age ankle- and calf-length boots have been in and out of vogue ever since he showed them.

Current designers continue to set the pace through fruitful cooperation with top shoe designers. Lagerfeld and Montana have worked with Walter Steiger; Givenchy with René Mancini; Gaultier with Stéphane Kélian; Lacroix with Sidonie Larizzi and Lolita Lempicka with Camille Unglik. Shoe designers of this calibre, though they produce collections of their own, respond to the creativity of people like Jean-Paul Gaultier, the Picasso of fashion, who dismembers clothes and reassembles them apparently at random, or Romeo Gigli, whose exercises in orientalism and medievalism have inspired copies of his jeweled troubador footwear worldwide, or John Galliano, who has taken styles from several periods of history to create fresh shapes and extraordinary heels.

Boot for Raquel Welch by Manolo Blahnik, 1974

# THE MASTERS: BLAHNIK

*Few women are immune to the charm of Manolo Blahnik's shoes. What they find irresistible is their extreme femininity and provocative sauciness. A Blahnik shoe is a concoction of rococo lightness, extrovert dash and worldly panache. It is essentially a fashion item because Blahnik is, himself, essentially a fashion designer. He would have been equally successful as a couturier or milliner. This is what distinguishes him from most other shoe designers working today and gives him the same standing as Perugia and Vivier in their prime.*

*Fashion intelligence is a rarity and in shoemakers is found only very occasionally. This does not mean that the lack of it prevents the designer from creating beautiful and exciting shoes; it merely means that he is a specialist. Manolo Blahnik is nothing so narrow. He is able to work with dress designers (as well as producing his own collections) for the same reason that Vivier was able to combine his creativity so successfully with Dior's – he is sufficiently attuned to the zeitgeist of the moment to be able to understand what must come next. Combine that with an endless flow of imaginative ideas and you have a world figure.*

Hand made Thong sandal.

Manolo Blahnik ©

Saint Gall lace and silk satin underneath – winter 1987-88

# OLD AND NEW LOOKS

The fashionable silhouette has altered regularly during this century. Bosoms have come and gone – and then come back again. Skirts have moved up and down to expose and cover the knee, but the ankle and foot have remained in view despite all the vagaries of fashion. Even before World War I, a low satin pump trimmed with a bow was allowed to peep from beneath the skirt. The twenties saw a new emphasis on shoes. They became decorative fashion items in themselves, with a character independent of the rest of fashion. They have maintained this independence ever since, which perhaps explains why the New Look, which had such an immediate impact on all aspects of fashion, hardly had any influence on the design of shoes.

1911

1914

c. 1935

1921

1924

1945

1948

Shoe by the Japanese designer Issey Miyake,
Paris Collection, 1988-89

# THE FASHION SHOE

*The fashion designer is a modern creation. When Charles Frederick Worth opened his fashion house on the rue de la Paix in 1858 he changed the designer's status from that of a mere dressmaker or man milliner to that of an arbiter of taste. He very quickly became an autocrat of fashion and his attitude to his customers seems to modern eyes the height of dictatorial insensitivity. Where he led, others quickly followed. Poiret, Chanel and Schiaparelli were not noteworthy for their modesty.*

*Shoemakers had to wait a little longer before the favoured ones were able to become more famous than their products, as has been the situation with couturiers for many years. What they all benefit from just as much as their grand dressmaker colleagues is the fact that, thanks to Worth's pioneering work, they have total freedom to design however they please. Also, because fashion is now accessible to all, they are able to find a market for almost anything they design. To service the needs of a huge fashion-conscious market, shoe designers are always trying to extend the parameters of what is acceptable and, at the same time, recycling ideas that were not fully exploited in the past. A glance at the styles on this page will make clear the opportunity and variety open to shoemakers today. They and their customers have never had a better time.*

Shoe by the Dutch designer Jan Jansen, 1980s

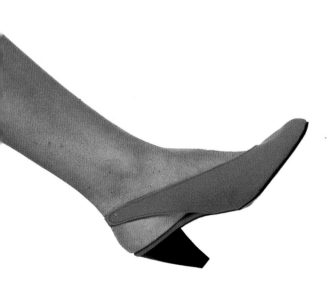

Bally shoe, Spring/Summer 1989

Platform sandals by the Italian firm of Fiorucci, 1970s

207

# HIGH HEELS

*The allure of high-heeled shoes is not merely that they make women look sexy in the eyes of many men. According to Beatrice Faust, author of* Women, Sex and Pornography, *they actually make them feel sexy, too. Faust maintains that high heels have a physiological effect by making the buttocks undulate twice as much and transmitting sexual sensations through the body.*

*That apart, high heels are equated by both men and women with glamour and sophistication. Christian Dior felt that they showed off his world-shattering New Look to best advantage and even the fact that many independently minded modern women prefer flat heels does not stop contemporary shoe designers like Johnny Moke and Trevor Hill from falling for them.*

*In the days of the most extreme form of high heel – the stiletto – there were often hazards, but because high heels flatter the ankles and make the legs look longer they will always have a following.*

The hazards of the stiletto heel, 1953

Christian Dior's New Look, 1947

Shoes by Johnny Moke (*front*) and Trevor Hill (*back*), 1988

Doc Martens in Trafalgar Square, London, 1988

Leather uppers at the Doc Marten factory, Woollaston, Northants, England

# THE DOC MARTENS STORY

*Doc Martens have brought the aggression of the storm-trooper to the suburbs in a way that would have horrified Dr Klaus Maertens, who invented the boot in 1945 as nothing more sinister than a step forward in comfort. Its air-cushioned sole was the important thing for him.*

*When Bill Griggs persuaded the German parent company to let him manufacture workmen's protective boots with the air-cushioned sole at his factory in Northampton, England, in 1960, he could have had no idea of the talismanic significance that DMs would assume as the uniform boot of the aggressively macho young urban male. British skinheads made it their own in the seventies. It was their 'bovver boot', with which they hoped to crush (or at least put the fear of God into) the complacent bourgeoisie. They failed to do so because the boot itself became tamed into an almost universal fashion accessory, even turning into the sort of shoe that college-educated boys in sports jackets and ties might wear for job interviews.*

*The paradox of the DM is the way in which it has been taken up by girls and gays to make statements far removed from those of the original skinheads. In the late eighties fashion has exploited the contrasts of mismatched items of clothing which are paired in such a way as to break all the accepted rules. London clubs have been full of girls in frilly net skirts and lace tops worn with DMs to temper the message of feminine frailty and vulnerability with a degree of toughness and self-reliance. The effect is ambivalent, just as it is when gay men wear DMs to project a masculinity which is possibly not what they actually feel. It is indicative of the confusion of roles and the blurring of distinctions that a boot with such down-to-earth origins should play such a central role in the semiotics of dress for well over a decade in many countries without losing any of its sexual potency.*

High fashion Doc Martens in patent leather by Johnny Moke, shown in *Vogue*, 1986, photograph by Demarchelier

# WACKY SOLES

*Shoe designers love fantasy – indeed, they are bound to. The very idea of designing shoes other than as basic protection for the foot is a fantasy in itself. The early Irish brogue, the original clog and the simple Egyptian sandal are the only styles of footwear that mankind needs in order to get along. Fortunately, man's creativity demands much more than the bare essentials of life to keep it fed and functioning. For that reason the history of footwear is one of endless conceits and fantasies, some wearable and some not. Many of the least practical are the most entertaining.*

*This century has been especially productive as far as fantasy shoes are concerned because technical advances and new materials have made the wildest dreams of shoemakers realizable even if, once made, they are not always wearable. When they are wearable the more bizarre creations not only feed the wearer's secret fantasies but also bring joy to the onlooker.*

*Left:* Vivienne Westwood, 'Rocking Horse Shoes', 1987

*Above:* Shoe fashion for second day of Royal Ascot, 1947

*Right:* John Moore shoes, 1988

*Far right:* Shoe, 1936

# THE YOUNG ONES

*The 1980s have witnessed a resurgence of interest in shoe design centred on the work of young designers trained in the traditional skills of the craft. Many of these designers actually produce their shoes by the old methods of the eighteenth-century cordwainers. Some insist on making them by hand and all resist the pressure to move into the world of mass-manufacture. The result is that their shoes are of a high level of workmanship and show an exemplary attention to detail. In going back to old methods, there is a risk of creating shoes that are more costume than fashion, but, at their best, the new young shoe designers combine the traditional strengths with the contemporary virtues of wit, freshness and relevance for the lives that their customers live today.*

*Top:* Willy van Rooy, 1988
*Above:* Emma Hope, 1988
*Left:* Johnny Moke, 1987
*Opposite:* Lola Pagola, 1988

Apart from designers and manufacturers and the styles they have produced, the twentieth century has been exceptional for the development of styles at street level. The extraordinary influence of sport and keep-fit activities has already been covered, but there are other developments that must be noted. Quite the biggest influence on shoe design, after sport, has been from the world of leisure activities. Shoes and boots for walking became popular during the wars. Tough and long-lasting, most of them were variations of the veldtshoen double construction that made footwear waterproof. The design was practical rather than fashionable: the main criterion was fitness of purpose, and much of the design know-how had been developed in the armed forces.

Workwear like Doc Martens had a great influence on leisure styles. The two came together in the United States in the Abingdon Shoe Company in Newmarket, New Hampshire. Owned by a Russian emigré called Nathan Swartz who had arrived in America in 1918, it was a small company, manufacturing workboots. Swartz's sons Herman and Sidney joined the business in the fifties and the firm prospered for the next decade by providing boots for companies to label as their own.

In the early seventies, increasing competition from cheaper Taiwanese and Korean products convinced the Swartz brothers that it was time to manufacture under their own label. Timberland boots were launched in 1975. Their image of the pioneer dream perfectly fitted the time. Ralph Lauren had already begun to make Americans nostalgic over their lost homesteader past. College students were reading Thoreau, wearing Levis and, when not in Weejuns (the Ivy League cult penny loafer), were putting on their Timberland boots. Young American men did not wish to look like Italians or Frenchmen. Bruce Weber was photographing dozens of them in America's wide-open spaces for the fashion magazine *G.Q.* – and, nine times out of ten, they would have Timberland boots on their feet to complete the image of the relaxed all-American macho male.

Timberland sales soared across America. In less than ten years, the company's production increased by more than 400 percent and annual sales nudged over the $100 million mark. Spectacular as it is, that development might have been predicted by the Swartz family. What took them completely by surprise was how such quintessentially American boots caught the imagination of young people all over the world. Their success was part of the rise in popularity since the late seventies of all things American. Nineteenth-century prairie life has found a loving audience in America for a long time – as the continued success of cowboy boots testifies. Thanks to blue jeans and Ralph Lauren and to films like *Butch Cassidy and the Sundance Kid* and *Paris, Texas*, clothing based on indigenous U.S. workwear has now become as glamorous to the rest of the world as jeeps and jukeboxes. In Italy, the Paninari, the affluent, young, urban middle classes, dress almost entirely in an American style, with jeans and Timberland boots as essential components of their fashion statement. Already, Timberlanders are history – like moccasins. They have been swallowed up in the mythology they have created.

Timberland boots are an example of the trend towards male interest in appearance. Women's fashion has always been based on the confidence that new looks can be promoted so strongly that all women will want them, but until the 1950s no such hopes could be entertained in menswear. Postwar social alienation and the impact of pop music changed the situation in the early fifties with the emergence of the first of the fashion 'crazes' for men, shoes known as brothel creepers or beetle crushers. The appeal of brothel creepers lay in their deliberate crudeness. Leather or suede uppers were sewn to crepe soles which at the peak of the craze could be as thick as two inches. The name spells out the sexuality of the shoe. They were a celebration of unsubtle masculinity and were the working-class counterpart of the desert boot – traditional officer wear in the Desert campaign – which had translated to civilian streets as 'smooth' middle-class footwear. Brothel creepers were as aggressive as desert boots were urbane. Even at the time, they were deliberately kitsch, part of the Teddy-boy fancy dress that included drainpipe trousers and draped-jacket zoot suits. When they were resurrected by young 'clubbers' in the mid-eighties, with fake fur, chains and imitation crocodile skins, they had become even more self-conscious exercises in contrived bad taste.

After such a weighty style, it was inevitable that fashion would swing to the extreme of narrowness and it did, in the form of the winkle-picker, or needlepoint, shoe. Again, a young urban working-class style, winkle-pickers were part of the uniform of a fifties sub-cult called the Mods. The Mod boys rode motor scooters and dressed precisely, lacking the menace of the brothel-creeper boys. Winkle-pickers were a restatement of the medieval long-toed poulaine, tempered for modern practicality.

Winkle-picker, 1960s

The fashion for pointed toes began in Italy, but the home of young fashion at this time was London, and that is where the style came to full fruition. The winkle-picker's appeal, like the poulaine's, lay in the sexuality of the pointed toe. As the fashion reached its peak, the heels began to rise and the points began to be smoothed off. The heels continued to grow until the Beatle boot had been created.

Given the hysterical adulation that surrounded the Merseyside pop group, an item of their costume as sexual as a shoe was bound to be copied. Just as Mod gear had appealed to young men who wanted to be taken as 'smart', so the Beatle boot was essential wear for anyone who considered himself 'with it'. Unlike the cowboy boots that were to have a resurgence of popularity some years later, Beatle boots were not at all 'butch' and resembled nothing more closely than the Victorian female buttoned boot.

Beatle boot, 1964

In fact, the Beatle boot was, if not an effeminate style, certainly a non-aggressive one. It had the bland acceptability of the group who introduced it. The swing away from its rather prissy style led in the 1970s to the Doc Marten boot which, like the brothel creeper, was aggressively anarchist and found a following in disaffected urban youth in Northern Europe and Great Britain. It has become associated with violence, extreme bigotry and crude nationalism to such an extent that many young men for whom it had been almost essential as a working boot abandoned it and turned to Timberland-style footwear which has no anti-social connotations.

One of the dreariest materials to emerge in men's fashion since World War II must surely be brushed pigskin, first introduced in the U.S. in 1957 and quickly used to make a series of middle-of-the-road shoes so utterly lacking in character that they found instant success with the middle-class male, who still wears them today. Marketed under the name of Hush Puppies, brushed pigskin has proved one of the most successful materials in the history of shoes.

Men's fashions since the war have largely reflected the nuances of the changing male image. Women's shoe styles have reflected their developing position in society. Much more so than in men's footwear, women's shoe fashion in the twentieth century has ranged across the centuries for inspiration. Designers have borrowed styles from all periods, but have usually managed successfully to translate these into the fashion mood of the times.

In the first years of the twentieth century, and lasting for some women almost up to the 1920s, the buttoned boot was the strongest female fashion, crossing all class boundaries. It was a triumph of practicality. With the exception of cheap versions made for working-class women, it kept feet warm and dry and ankles supported.

In the twenties, women assumed some of the trappings of emancipation but somewhat less of the reality. High boots largely disappeared, though in the early years of the decade knee-high Russian boots had a brief vogue. These were so immediately popular that they quickly lost the essence of a fashionable look – to make those who do not have it envy and hope to emulate those who do.

The real style of the twenties was the low-cut shoe with the curved louis heel, fastened by buttoned or buckled bar straps across the instep. This was not an emancipated as much as a sexless style, as were the flapper dress and short hair of the period. Fashion historians frequently point out that due to the enormous carnage of World War I, twenties girls dressed to fill the gap left by the lost young men. The clothes of the period simply do not bear this out. The trauma of the war turned women into the children, male and female, that had been lost to the war. If they can be taken to symbolize anything, it is surely the innocence that war had destroyed.

By the time the thirties were well underway and the effects of the 1929 Crash had been absorbed, the fashionable female image had swung from gamine to siren, with Jean Harlow and Joan Crawford as the new archetypes. Just as actresses had led the field at the turn of the century, so they did now. The only difference was one of impact. Hollywood stars were seen by billions of people who were instantly exposed to the styles of their favourites. In shoes this meant high heels, often in sensuous suede, with sling backs, peep-toes and ankle straps: the full armoury of seductive footwear. Stars of the style of Mae West projected the confidence of women who were equal to men in that their sexuality had to be taken into account. They explode the modern myth that women in flat shoes are more likely to be treated as equals by men than those in high heels. But the flat-shoe approach was also part of the Hollywood picture, exemplified by Katharine Hepburn, the paradigm of the sporty, independent new woman.

Fashion is one of the early victims of war. Moralists come into their own, frivolity is outlawed, restrictions are imposed. World War II had an effect on shoes in that shortage of materials meant that traditional leather-soled shoes were hardly available; new clothing was rationed and craftsmen were drafted. The results were predictable. Apart from the development of wedge heels and platform soles – imposed more by the limitations of the material than by a design vision – the look of the late thirties prevailed. The New Look of 1947 brought no corresponding breakthrough in shoe style. The elegant court pump, kept rather plain, was the standard shoe of the time. Although Perugia created fantasy styles based on turn-of-the-century spats and buttoned leggings, they did not venture beyond the confines of *haute couture*.

The fifties witnessed what might prove to be the last flowering of female glamour. Balmain, Balenciaga and Chanel were dressing their private customers

Court shoe in brown crocodile
with high stiletto heel,
Ferragamo, 1958

luxuriously, but with a refinement not seen since Captain Molyneux in the thirties. Shoes became correspondingly understated and, as the decade advanced, the pared-down minimalism of the shape became elongated at the toe. The pointed toe required a correspondingly delicate heel. The stiletto was invented, and inaugurated a style as carefully balanced and structured as a piece of sculpture. The Italians created the stiletto and it reflects their brio, style and sheer audaciousness of invention. It was worn by all fashionable Western women – frequently at great cost to the environment. A woman of average height exerts two tons of weight per square inch on a stiletto heel.

The stiletto continued into the sixties, long after the pointed toe had been superseded by other treatments, and was only slowly phased out. New designers like Mary Quant, Emmanuelle Khanh and Betsey Johnson brought the heel down and the flat, ballet-style pump, of the kind worn in the mid-nineteenth century for ballroom dancing, became the no-fuss, go-anywhere shoe that appealed to the unique new fashion class: people under thirty who had style and the money to indulge it. The 'swinging' sixties were a period of simplicity in footwear. As the momentum of the decade increased, the fashion that emerged as universally appealing was the boot. Short, mid-calf, wide, narrow – it was everywhere. Made of plastic as well as leather, in brilliant colours or in the white of the sixties, it could be sexy or demure – it was a fashion that could be all things to all women.

Boots were still popular in the seventies but in a style cut closer to the leg and usually with a high heel. The sixties had been a decade of momentous movements in fashion; the seventies continued their restlessness – looks and moods came and went with bewildering speed. Designers were pragmatic and eclectic, picking up on movements at street level, plundering historic styles and unearthing ethnic looks from all parts of the world. The unifying element of the decade was found in footwear. Heavy platform soles came and went, but the clumpy shoe or boot with a solid stacked heel remained. Designers and individual craftsmen played every possible decorative variation with materials and trims in order to explore all avenues of bad taste and vulgarity. The seventies were a desolate decade for fashion because judgment was constantly overridden by enthusiasm. In the scramble to express individual personality, the perimeters of disciplined design were constantly breached and the results were completely lacking in style.

The early eighties saw the biggest fashion shock since the mini. It came from a new wave of Japanese designers in Paris and from the street fashion of London which had been channelled into a 'look' by fashion students. It was Punk, postmodernism, anarchy or honesty, depending upon your age and viewpoint. It erased the jumble of styles which had confused the last years of the seventies.

The new look was as universal as the black which all designers featured every season until the middle of the decade. Its effect on shoes was instant. The extravagant shapes and colours went – in their place came simple black shoes with no heels. These were modelled on Chinese and Japanese peasant shoes and appealed equally to the ultra-fashionable of both sexes. Together with the flat-heeled pump, these shoes may eventually come to symbolize the spirit of the decade. As yet, it is too early to judge and there are other contenders: the spiky high heels that accompanied the Christian Lacroix style of dressing; the Doc Marten boot which has been a constant fashion with certain young women for the last decade, and the romantic costume shoe, complete with buckles and bows, reintroduced by the new-wave London shoe designers.

# ACKNOWLEDGMENTS

No book on shoes, no matter how slight, can be embarked upon without consulting the doyenne of shoe scholarship, June Swann, until recently Keeper of the Shoe Collection at Northampton Museum, England. My debt to her is considerable. Apart from the advice she gave me, she was kind enough to read the manuscript before it went to the printer, as did her successor at Northampton, Andrew McKay. They both made valuable suggestions that I was able to incorporate into the final text.

I would like to thank the Bally Schuhmuseum of Schonenwerd, Switzerland; the Clarks of Street Museum, Street, England; the Librarian and staff of Cordwainers Technical College, London, England, and the staff of the Fashion Institute of Technology in New York and of the Victoria and Albert Museum in London.

Peter Schweiger of James Taylor & Co. and Oliver Sweeney of McAfee – two of London's few remaining bespoke shoemakers – gave me valuable information concerning the technical aspects of making shoes by hand and Sir Edward Rayne kindly gave me the benefit of his many years of experience in the shoe trade. Jill Edmonds, William Evans, Judy Rumbold, Robert Stewart, Marina Sturdza and Brian Williams provided me with information at various points. To them, and to other friends who have helped and encouraged, my thanks.

The publishers would like to thank the following for their help in the preparation of this book, and in particular the designers and companies who generously made available original sketches and photographs from their archives:

Agence Prestige, Christine Ahrens, Marilyn Anselm, David Bailey, Bally of Switzerland, G.H. Bass and Co., Susan Bennis and Warren Edwards, Dirk Bikkembergs, Manolo Blahnik, Debbie Bourne at Lynn Franks, Robert Clergerie, Andrew Collyer, Brown Company, André Courrèges, Patrick Cox, Michael Cummins, Anita Davis, Christian Dior, Christian Dorley-Brown, David Evans, Ferragamo, Katharina Feuchtinger at John Lobb, Fiorucci, Jean-Paul Gaultier, Gucci, Diana Hinton, Emma Hope, Jan Jansen, Allen Jones, Charles Jourdan, Ralph Lauren, Steven Lopez at the Natural Shoe Store, Peter Hope Lumley, Andrew McKay, Regina Martino, Lisa Milroy, Johnny Moke, Condé Nast Publications, Robert Opie, Lola Pagola, Cindy Palmano, Andrea Pfister, Mary Quant, Paco Rabanne, Juan Ramos, Paula Rego, Karen Reilly at Cordwainers Technical College, Russell & Bromley, Nina Schultz, Vanessa Shaw at H & M Rayne, Per Spook, Damian Stephens; Swaine, Adeney, Briggs & Sons; Willy van Rooy, Roger Vivier and Kelly Webb-Lamb

# PHOTOGRAPHIC ACKNOWLEDGMENTS

(Abbreviations: t–top, b–bottom, l–left, r–right, c–centre.)

Christine Ahrens 199. Amsterdam, National Vincent van Gogh Foundation/National Museum Vincent van Gogh 69. *Arena* 82-83. Bally Shoes 163tr, 206-207. Bally Shoe Museum, Schönwerd 12, 13, 43t, 44br, 52b, 58t, 98b, 90bc, 90br, 111c, 111b, 163. Bath Museum of Costume 205bl. Susan Bennis/Warren Edwards 20t, 20b. Dirk Bikkembergs 72, 164-165, 172tl, 173b. Manolo Blahnik 23, 67bl, 67br, 201, 202-203. Suzanne Bosman 85, 119b. Henry Bourne for ELLE 185, 206bl. British Film Institute/National Film Archive 76l, 76r, 80-81, 81, 84, 84-85, 89bl, 90, 91, 95t, 125c, 152l, 152r, 153, 158, 159, 162t, 166, 168. Brown Company 162b. Brussels, Musées Royaux de Belgique 56. Budapest, Museum of Fine Art 126t. Alfa Castaldi 111tr. Cecil Sharp Folk Dance Society 156t, 157bl. Chantilly, Musée Condé (photo Giraudon) 117c. Clarks 26. Robert Clergerie 192. Columbia Pictures Corporation (photos National Film Archive) 76r, 84, 84-85. © Condé Nast Publications Ltd 55b, 120b, 122-123, 132r, 148b, 176, 186, 211. Copenhagen, Dansk Folkemuseum 128b. Courrèges 132tl. Courtauld Institute, Conway Library 50tr. Patrick Cox 216. Dior 205br, 208b. Kim van Dooren 214r. Christian Dorley-Brown 45c, 210b. Courtesy David Evins (photos Eileen Tweedy) 20-21, 21t, 21c, 21b, 154-155. English Heritage, The Iveagh Bequest, Kenwood 22, 108br. English Heritage, Rangers House 116b. Ferragamo 106-107, 110, 121tl, 182, 188-189, 220. Fiorucci 207b. Gucci 118tl, 118bl. Hulton Picture Company 55t, 89br, 92, 92-93, 93tr, 94, 105, 120t, 126bl, 126br, 127t, 127b, 128t, 134bl, 136, 163b, 171b, 173t, 205tl, 205tr, 208t, 212t, 213r. Hulton Picture Company/Bettmann Archive 80l. Martin Hurlimann 50br. Jan Jansen 166bl, 166br, 207t. Courtesy Allen Jones 70, 77, 78. Norma Kamali 149. Kobal Collection 95br, 174-175. Ralph Lauren 118br. Erica Lennard 115. Liverpool, Walker Art Gallery 51tr. London: Museum of London 30, 33, National Gallery, 53, 109, National Portrait Gallery 130b, Victoria and Albert Museum 134tl, Victoria and Albert Museum (photos Eileen Tweedy) 34t, 49b, 132bl, 133l, 187t, 187b, Victoria and Albert Museum (Theatre Museum) 111tl, 146l, 150t, 150b, 151, Wallace Collection 118-119. London

Features 167. Mansell Collection 42b, 47t, 60, 108tl, 108bl, 117bl, 121tr, 131b, 148t, 204tl, 204tr. McAfee Shoes 125t, 125b. © Robert Mapplethorpe, Courtesy Art + Commerce (Photographed for STERN Magazine) 79. Regina Martino 66bl. MGM/United Artists Entertainment Company (photos National Film Archive) 90-91, 95, 162l, 168. Johnny Moke 112b, 214bl. New York, Fashion Institute of Technology, Edward C. Blum Design Laboratory. Gift of Richard Martin (photo Irving Solero) 67tl. New York, Metropolitan Museum of Art, Gift of Capezio Inc. 10. Metropolitan Museum of Art, Havemeyer Collection 147. Northampton Museum and Art Gallery 29, 32, 35r, 44bl, 45, 99, 138, 139, 142b, 218t, 218b. Courtesy Claes Oldenburg 169b. Robert Opie 133r. Oxford, Ashmolean Museum 42t. Tim Page 134-135, 135. Lola Pagola 215. Cindy Palmano 17, 66r. Pancaldi 204b. Paramount Pictures (photos National Film Archive) 158, 159. Paris: Bibliothèque Nationale, Cabinet des Estampes (photo Giraudon) 31t, Musée d'Orsay (photo Giraudon) 94-95, Musée du Louvre (photo Giraudon) 96, 134tr, Musée du Petit Palais (photo Archives Photographiques) 48r. Andrea Pfister 114t, 114b, 117br. Popperfoto 46tl, 50tl, 90bl, 121c, 121br, 160. Press Association, London 93b, 167tl, 170b, 171t, 172-173. Agence Prestige, Paris (photos Daniel Angeli/Laurent Sola) 18-19, 190t, 190bl, 190br, 191. Private Collections 67tr, 68, 70, 116t, 130t. Mary Quant 73. Paco Rabanne 47b. Courtesy Juan Ramos 74l, 74r, 75. Reims, Musée des Beaux-Arts 44t. Michael Roberts 41. Rome, Capitoline Museum (photo Anderson/Alinari) 16. Willy van Rooy 214tl. Royal Academy of Dance 145. Saatchi Collection 71. Nina Schultz 73b, 209, 212b, 213. Brian Schuel 156b, 157. Edwin Smith 51, 129. Daniel Sorine 146r. Per Spook 54t. Chris Steele-Perkins/Magnum 161. Phil Stern 169t. Stockholm, Moderna Museet 65. Stuttgart, Landesbibliothek 46b. Laurence Sudre/Distribution VU 131t. Venice, Museo Civico (photo Alinari) 49t. Vienna, Kunsthistorisches Museum 52t. Roger Viollet 122. Roger Vivier 112-113, 183. Warner Bros. (photo National Film Archive) 81. Paul Yule 210t.

From T. Wright, *The Romance of the Shoe*, 1922, 35l, 36, 37t, 37b, 58b, 98t.

# INDEX